What good do you think

Foreword

This is a book about my experience while detained at Her Majesty's pleasure. Many a book has been written about the violent environment of a prison, an environment of despair and little hope. This book is not about that. This book looks at a serious subject, but with humour. My aim is to show a different side to prison life, a lighter side. This is a story about individuals, characters and personalities. It's also a story about a system that does not work, and how a person with no experience of criminality or prison got through it. This book isn't even about me. It is about the people I met, some good people who made mistakes like I did. I believe there is no such thing as a bad person, just a person who has made bad choices.

<u>The names of the people in this book have been changed to protect the guilty.</u>

Chapter 1

Getting nicked

"Every saint has a past, and every sinner has a future." Oscar Wilde

I am lying on my bed. It is 8am, and I have been up all night, cocaine not allowing me to sleep. I am on the phone with my ex, Kelly, who is in Australia; the positive of having friends in Oz is you have someone to talk to at 6am when you are off your box. I am trying to get her to send me some dirty pictures and I am wanking away like a Duracell bunny. I think I hear my front door open, but then I think it's the cocaine making me paranoid. I live alone.

Two blokes walk into my bedroom. Stab-proof vests and North Face jackets: the uniform for undercover cops. Even I know that. My cock in one hand and my mobile in the other, I freeze. They look at with me with disgust. The cheek of it. You walk into my bedroom unannounced, and I am in the wrong? "Are there any weapons in the house?! Is anyone else here with you?!" I don't know what the fuck is going on. I still have my cock in my hand. I hang up the phone to Kelly. She must think I shot my load and just hung up on her. All I can stutter is a confused "No" to their questions. My mind can't even fathom what they are asking. The coppers are arguing about who is going to put handcuffs on me. One of the coppers asks me if there is anything in the house that should not be there, and the thought hits me that I have a couple of grams of gear on the table from last night's excesses. As I am sat on the edge of my bed, I can see loads of coppers coming into my flat. I ask the copper if they have a warrant: I have seen people ask that on the TV. He tells me he does not need one because they have 'probable cause' as they believe there are drugs in the property. In my head I am thinking, "Shit, I should have finished that gear off." I am trying to be calm, thinking, "All this for a bit of Percy."

After about fifteen minutes a shout comes from my kitchen: "Here we go, Gov. Fuck me—it is going to be a good Christmas party this year." The copper who has been asking me random questions leaves the room, then comes back in and asks, "Whose drugs are they in the kitchen?" I don't say anything: again, I have seen this on the TV. He stands me up and walks me to my kitchen. They really went to work on my kitchen; shit everywhere. I am thinking, "Them bastards better clean this shit up."

Standing in my kitchen they show me five boxes on my counter, which look like VHS cassettes, wrapped in Clingfilm. They are kilos of cocaine!! I am stunned. My first reaction is: they put that there! "This is a stitch up, you cunts!" is the only thing I manage to say. The copper who was first through the door – proper smug twat – reads me my rights: "I am arresting you for possession with intent to supply Class A drugs. Anything you say will be used in a court of law against you."

They take me to my living room. Sit me down and start grilling me. "This is ten years in prison; whose drugs are they?! You are in a lot of trouble son, you need to start thinking about your future." I ignore all the questions, mainly because I have a million things running through my head, including a couple of grams of cocaine and a lot of alcohol. One of the coppers picks up a picture of my two kids and puts it on the table in front of me and says, "Think about them. Tell me whose drugs they are." This gives me the right hump. I shoot him a stare and tell him to piss off. A copper observes the empty bottle of Jack Daniels and six Stella cans on the table and asks who was drinking with me the night before. That was my nightcap. I got home drunk.

After they search the rest of my flat, turning it upside down, most of the coppers start to file out with evidence bags that are mostly full of electronics. I think: the copper who gets to go through my mobile will get an eyeful of the pictures on it. Behind my sofa is a laptop in a steel case that my uncle gave me, a KGB-looking thing that he got off the market. That would bend their minds. But somehow they missed it. I still have it to this day. I wish the gear had been hidden in that.

The smug copper is still with me, trying to make chit-chat, asking me about boxing as I have some memorabilia in my flat. At this point I am just ignoring him. This other copper, who is a fucking massive, six foot five, protein-sniffing, retarded-looking fucker, asks the smug copper if he has "done it yet?" I am taken to my kitchen. The drugs are still on the counter, and they are taking loads of pictures. The big copper picks up a kilo and asks if I have ever seen it before. I say I genuinely haven't, and I have no idea how it got there. At this point he thrusts it at my stomach and, instinctively, I grab it. The copper says, "OK, you don't want to talk, so you have fucked yourself. Once we get to the station it will be too late to talk." I put the kilo down. They allow me to get dressed, and ask me if I want to take anything with me to the station. I say, "Yeah, I need my Arsenal membership card. I am going to the Arsenal v Wigan game tonight." They both laugh out loud. One says he'll quit his job if I get to go to the match. I insist, and off I go to the police station with my Arsenal membership card, a massive hangover, and an arrest for conspiracy to supply five kilos of cocaine.

I ask which police station they are taking me to, because there is one I do not want to go to as I am often there for work. They ask me about my job, and I tell them I am a support worker for people who are homeless in Hammersmith and Fulham. They say they are taking me to Chiswick, which I think is a touch, as I am thinking it will be quiet, full of drink-driving bankers; and I'm glad it's not Hammersmith, where I often need to advocate for my clients. I might see a client there, which would take some explaining.

At the station, some copper behind a massive desk asks me questions about how I am feeling. How do you think you?! I tell him I had a skinful the night before and I am on anti-depressants and I am tired. He asks if I want to see a nurse. I never did finish my wank, but I decline. I ask him if I get a phone call. I have seen that on the TV too. He says yes and asks who I want to call. I say my mate John, who I am meeting at Holloway Road station to go watch the Arsenal, to let him know I might be late and to not wait for me. Again, they find this funny. I am asked if I have legal representation; I say no, and they say a duty solicitor will be allocated to my case.

I get the impression they don't believe the drugs they found are not mine.

First, they want to take my fingerprints, DNA swab, a drugs test, and some mug shots (quite an apt term for my situation). I am taken to a cell, and asked to leave my shoes outside, like they have had a new carpet fitted or something. I think most people walking into a cell when it is their first time ever in one would feel overwhelmed. I just want a kip. I haven't slept and the fuckers took my cocaine off me. I am woken up some time later to be interviewed. I have no idea what time it is. Some eager copper who is about twelve asks me how I am feeling. "Much better now I have had a kip thanks, slept like a baby" is not the answer he's expecting, going by the gormless look on his face.

I am taken to a room to meet my solicitor. He asks very little except have I been convicted of an offence before. I say no, I have never been arrested. I presume he feels the same way as I do; the drugs are obviously not mine. As he reads over my charge sheet he says, "Nothing to worry about." He encourages me to say "No comment" to every question in the interview and he tells me I will get out on bail. This is all I want at this point.

I am escorted to an interview room; I am to be interviewed by the smug copper and another copper I didn't see at my flat. While they are setting up, one of the coppers tells my solicitor and me they need to keep the window closed because someone climbed out of it during a break in interview and was found in the McDonald's across the road. The window is six foot off the floor and is four by one. A tape recorder makes a loud beeping noise and I am reminded that I am under arrest. I hadn't forgotten. I have the transcript of the questions I was asked during interview, with my "No comment" reply to every one. This is important when you are in prison, I later discover.

I am asked similar questions as at my flat. "If the drugs are not yours, tell me whose drugs they are?" I confidently say, "No comment." There is a series of the same question put in different ways, tone and manner. The smug copper who arrested me says, "If we have this wrong, explain the situation and we will investigate it." This question throws me, as I presumed they would do this anyway. One question stands out. "Who are Patrick O'Neil and John McDowell?" I haven't got a fucking clue what they are talking about and I say, "No comment." I can tell the coppers are getting frustrated. I want a McDonald's now. They terminate the interview and I am taken back to my cell. I am on a serious comedown now; my nose is streaming, and I am sweating like a bastard.

After a couple of hours more sleep they want to interview me again. I think this a bit weird. I can't understand why they would want to hear me say "No comment" twenty more times. It turns out this is the big reveal: they show me their cards. They tell me they had been following Patrick

O'Neil and John McDowell and they had intercepted them on the street outside my flat. They had a key to my flat in their possession. They had tried every door in my block, and my door opened, and they discovered five kilos of cocaine. I am waiting for them to tell me how O'Neil and McDowell got a key to my flat, but they were looking to me to provide the answer. I have absolutely no idea who they are. In my head, I am beginning to put things together, but no way am I telling them what I'm thinking. They show me pictures of Patrick O'Neil and John McDowell, and the penny drops. My heart sinks. I met them, once, in a pub, friends of friends. I know them by their nicknames, Paddy and Jock. My mind is racing. I realise I could be in the shit here, but I keep telling myself, you are not involved in this, it will be OK. I am thinking, just get out on bail, and sort this mess out.

I am returned to the cell again. Now there is some nutter in the cell next door to me shouting about Jesus. I want to join him to be honest; I could do with some help from above. A copper comes into my cell soon after. He tells me they can keep me in custody for twenty-four hours before they must charge or release me. He tells me he has applied for an extension, as the investigation is still ongoing. He explains this has been granted. I am not sure if this is positive or not, but I am thinking they have had a look at their surveillance, and my phone, and cannot connect me to this and are reluctant to charge me and then look a bit stupid. The smug copper comes in my cell and sits next to me like he is a caring mate. "I don't think you realise how much trouble you are in; you need to start talking." To be honest, this makes me think I have the upper hand and he is desperate. All I say is, "I am not involved in this; if you investigate it you will see that." He looks pissed off now and says, "You are fucking yourself, can't say I didn't try." I don't know why he is pissed off; I am just encouraging him to do his job.

I am woken in the night and brought back to the massive desk. I am told I am being charged with 'Conspiracy to supply Class A drugs." I am then told I am to be remanded in custody until I appear in court tomorrow. I am pissed off and look at my solicitor and remind him he said I would be getting out on bail. He says, "I did not know it was five kilos of drugs." I am asked if I would now like to make a call. They suggest I don't call my mate John.

I call my dad, explain I have been arrested because some drugs were found in my flat, but not to worry, they are not mine. I am told I cannot talk about the case against me, which I don't understand. I ask my dad to come to Westminster Magistrates' Court in the morning, as I need him to help me to apply for bail. This is probably the hardest phone call I have ever had to make. I feel really deflated. I feel I have let my family down.

The copper behind the desk asks me if I have any questions. I say, "Yeah, what is the Arsenal score?"

Back in the cell again, I am trying to work out how much shit I am in and how I can get out of it. I must get bail. If not, I am fucked! I need to speak to people to find out how I am wrapped up in this. I feel if I can get bail, I can prove my innocence. Now this is where it gets tricky. Am I innocent? Not by a long shot. Am I guilty of the charge against me? I don't think so. Am I? Put it this way: Did someone say, "Dave, can I put five kilos of cocaine in your flat?" And did I reply: "Yeah, mate, no bother, crack on."?

This did not happen. Who would agree to that?! My head tells me that common sense will prevail and all this will be sorted out.

The next morning, I am escorted to Westminster Magistrates' Court. As I leave my cell a copper tells me Arsenal beat Wigan two-nil and says, "Up the Gunners." In the police van prisoners are kept apart from each other in little cells, so we can't see each other. But I can hear two people talking, and I am pretty sure they are Paddy and Jock. I don't say a word and I try to listen. I hear one say, "They nicked Dave." They shout my name, but I ignore them. I could do with speaking to them, but I am not having a conversation in a van with police listening. One by one they take us out of the van and into the holding cells at the court. They put Paddy, Jock and me into the same big holding cell.

"What the fuck is going on?" I ask.

They are reluctant to talk now, as they say there are listening devices in the cells. This seems convenient, and a convenient way of not answering me. They are very relaxed, even jovial. The only thing they ask me is if I said anything in my interview. I say no. I am not sure they believe me; they certainly don't trust me, which is fucking funny in this situation.

A court officer comes to the cell and gives us each a bib, like we are off for a game of five-a-side football. We are taken to small glass-walled rooms to meet our solicitors. I ask mine why I am attending court with the other two. He informs me that we are appearing together as part of a conspiracy. I tell him I don't even know them. He tells me we need to concentrate on getting bail. He tells me my dad is at the court; they have spoken, and he will provide anything needed for a bail request. They have put my parents' home as the bail address, which makes sense. I ask him what the chances of me getting bail are, and he says it's a serious charge, but he has made a good application and is hopeful. I am taken back to the big cell with the other two. One is telling the other that his brief is the nuts, who works on big drug cases. They advise me to get my own brief and to drop my appointed one, as they don't give a shit. I have no idea how they expect me to pay for my own brief. Do they work on credit?

We are taken up to the court. We all look a bloody mess. I see my dad. I can't make eye contact with him; it would break me, and I need to concentrate. I am told I will be asked to stand and give my name and address to the judge when prompted. People in suits start to pile into the court, the judge comes out of a little door at the back, and everyone stands. One by one we provide our names and addresses. Someone starts to talk, who I am guessing is the counsel for the Crown Prosecution Service. She starts to outline the details of my arrest and charges. She adds that I tested positive for cocaine in custody; I definitely can't look at my dad now. The judge says he cannot deal with this and we need to go to Crown Court. I am thinking, sweet, if you can't deal with this, then I can go home. I still don't see the point of appearing at a Magistrates' Court for the sake of it, knowing they can't deal with it. No wonder the court system is so slow. Each of our barristers says they want to apply for bail. They hear Paddy's and Jock's applications. My chance to apply comes and my solicitor talks about my father being there and how I will be reliable to return to court as I am working full time, have accommodation, two children, and have submitted my passport to the court. The CPS barrister stands and says, "Your honour, these men were involved in a conspiracy to supply £1.9 million pounds of uncut cocaine, and they are a flight risk."

HOW FUCKING MUCH?!

The judge does not even think about it. "Bail denied, you will remain in custody until you appear at an assigned Crown Court."

I am going to prison.

I am trying to front it out; show I am not about to fucking cry. Shoulders back, head up. I think, OK Dave, you can do a couple of weeks in prison, just keep your head down.

Below the court we can see our solicitors. Mine apologises and says he tried his best to get bail, but they would never bail all three of us, or just one of us. Guilty by association. He says he will come to the prison; I will be going to Wandsworth. Close to home at least. He says he will get a visit to start our defence. I ask how long all this will take. "A few months." WHAT? Is he fucking joking? How can I go to prison for a few months for something I have not done or been found guilty of? The only evidence they have is the drugs they found in my house, which they cannot link me to. I can only imagine how white I have gone. My solicitor puts his hand on my shoulder and says, "Don't worry, prison is not that bad". I wonder how much time he has he done in prison?

I never see him again.

Chapter 2

Wanno

"Like a river that don't know where it's flowing. I took a wrong turn and I just kept going." Bruce Springsteen

Travelling to HMP Wandsworth in a SERCO prison van, I am put in a cell, which is more like a plastic coffin, with a small blacked out window. No seat belt. I suppose if we crash there is so little space in the cell it wouldn't do much damage to you. You would think the atmosphere would be sullen, but not at all. It's like we're heading to Butlin's for a lads holiday. People are singing and laughing. Personally, I am not in the mood for a singsong. I am devastated. I am trying to go through the thoughts racing through my head, one thing at a time. I am going to be in prison for at least a couple of months. What does this mean for my flat, my job, financially? Will I be sacked? Will I lose my flat, as I can't pay the rent? What the hell am I going to tell my sons? I don't feel too sorry for myself, but I am worried what this will do to my family.

I shout out to Paddy and Jock, "What the fuck is going on? Someone needs to step up here, how the fuck am I on my way to prison?"

Jock shouts back, "Don't worry, you'll need to do a bit of bird, but it'll be fine, you'll be walking soon."

This is a relief to me, as this suggests that someone is going to step up and say, "Dave isn't anything to do with this," and after the police look into it they will realise I am not part of a conspiracy and I will be released, maybe get a lesser charge and 'Time served' at my next court appearance. My next thought is, "How the fuck am going to survive prison?!" I wonder if I would be attractive to any rapists.

The van pulls up outside the prison. It looks like a castle with a big wooden door and even has a flag on top. We wait outside for ages. The big doors open, and we drive into a courtyard. I can't even see the top of the big, stone walls from my little window, they are so high. The van pulls into another holding area and we again wait there for ages. Not that I am in any rush. After some time, I see a couple of officers come out of a portacabin with RECEPTION written above the door. The two officers walk towards the van. One by one, the doors of our little cells are opened and we are asked to go into reception. Everyone is still buoyant; people seem excited by the prospect of being locked in a cell. I feel like the only sane one in the asylum. We are called one by one to come to a reception desk. "You have been remanded in custody." I don't know why people keep telling me stuff I am unlikely to have forgotten about. He asks if I smoke, and I say no, but later learn I should have said yes. They take a picture of me. I look bloody awful. They issue me with a card with the picture on and a 'Prison Number' that they tell me I will need to be able to do anything, and to remember it or keep the card safe. The officers look pissed off and are miserable.

I am placed in a holding cell with all the other lads I came in with. They are no longer full of beans and the situation seems to have hit some of them. First, I am to see a nurse for a medical check. She only asks a few questions, makes no actual medical checks. I say I am taking anti-depressants and I need some soon as I am withdrawing. I inform her I have a pacemaker and I have a cardiology appointment in the community in two weeks. She says she has recorded it and asks if I am suicidal? I say no but request, in a light-hearted way, that she ask me again tomorrow. She tells me I will have a more thorough health check in a couple of days. (I never did). I am then ushered out of the room into another one. This is the security check. I am told to go into an open cubicle and strip. No curtain, just strip, in front of five officers. This now feels like the first real taste of having my liberty taken away. It is humiliating. I must turn around, bend over, spread my arse cheeks and cough. They check under my feet and inside my mouth. I am told I can get dressed again and I'm then asked to sit on a big grey plastic chair with BOSS on it. I ask what this is for. An officer tells me it is a metal detector to see if I have any contraband inside me. I tell him I have a pacemaker and ask if it is safe. He tells me to shut up. It makes a noise, so they ask me to stand and they get this big wand thing out and start to wave it at my bollocks and arse. I am quite a relaxed, calm person, but I can feel my anger building. I bite my tongue and stay quiet. I understand I am here to be punished (although at this point I am on remand and have not been found guilty of anything), but I don't understand his need to be a cunt. People are much more likely to adhere to instruction when asked politely than by someone being rude to them. I have been in prison for twenty minutes and I already hate the officers. I wonder if I am here as punishment, or for punishment.

Next, I am at the stores to be given my kit. Fuck me, the stuff given out is rank! I am given two thick blue T-shirts that are like belly tops. Long at the back and six inches shorter at the front with no shape at all to them. Two pairs of grey tracksuit bottoms that Sports Direct couldn't even shift. I am also given three pairs of blue boxers – I can't bring myself to look inside them – a towel like a poppadom; a couple of blue sheets (which are well pressed, to be fair), and an orange blanket, that stinks. I ask for a jumper as it is freezing. They tell me they don't have any left. I am wearing a pair of jeans and a polo T-Shirt. I tell myself I will just wear these clothes every day and wash them at night. No way I am wearing the gear they have given me. Luckily, what I am wearing is navy blue, as I am told you can't wear white or black, and nothing with zips, hoods or drawstrings. I cannot fathom why they have a colour dress code. An officer then asks me a series of questions.

Are you in a gang? No.

Are you a racist? No.

Have you ever committed arson? No.

Are you mentally unwell? Not yet.

He tells me this is a risk assessment to see if I am a risk to others.

I am given a 'non-smokers pack' which is a small bag containing tea, coffee, and a packet of biscuits. The smokers get a small pack of tobacco. I am the only one to say I don't smoke; the other lads look at me like I am stupid. Everyone says they smoke to get the tobacco, to trade it.

We are led as a group up to the induction wing. There is a large reception counter as we enter. It is manned by cons, which I find odd. The guy explains we will stay on the induction wing for a few days to acclimatise. The guy seems sound; he is patient and answers a lot of the questions people have. I am struggling to hear him as the noise is deafening. People shouting and banging on doors. He seems to know a lot of the lads coming in. One lad asks him if chip night is still on a Wednesday. He asks if it is anyone's first time inside. I say it is mine. I am the only one, or the only one who admits to it. He asks me if I have any questions, I say I have thousands, but for now, I just want to make a call. He tells me I will be given an envelope, and in this will be a code for two pounds phone credit that I can use on the prison phone. Paddy comes over and asks the guy to put me in a cell with someone decent. The guy says he has just the person, an older guy who knows the ropes and can help me get my head round the system, he came in on a 'Bus' just before me; he says he is quiet and a nice guy. I thank him and I think the prison should put him on at the main reception rather than the officers.

I am told I am on the 'twos', or second floor landing. Another guy who was at the reception area walks me to my cell. The landing is about the length of a football pitch with a door every six feet on both sides. There are two more levels up, and one down. I ask him when the officers will give me the phone credit so I can call home. "Don't call them officers, you melt, call them screws." He tells me the wing we are on is E-wing, but everyone calls it Beirut. That doesn't sound good...

I am shown my cell. My first reaction is how the fuck do two men live in such a small space? Looking back, it was one of the larger cells I was in. It was about twelve feet by eight feet. I am introduced to my 'padmate', Tony, who is in the cell. He seems cool. Late forties, slim guy with grey hair. He has bad teeth, but he doesn't seem to care. He shows me where I can put my stuff and tells me I am on the top bunk, which looks like it will collapse if I get on it. Tony and I have a chit-chat. He tells me I shouldn't ask people what they are in for. I haven't asked him, but he asks me. I am casual about it. "Drugs" seems to be the right response. He tells me he is in for burglary. He tells me it will be 'unlock' for grub, soon. I have hardly eaten in about forty-eight hours, but I am not hungry. I wonder what it will be like going to a big hall to eat dinner with a load of cons. On the TV this is usually where all the fights start; someone will try to take my pudding from me, and if I don't resist, I will be someone's bum bitch. I wonder if I can just not eat for a few months.

The door to the cell is unlocked and Tony tells me to come with him and bring my plate and bowl that were given to me with my kit, which are like something you would give a two-year-old. Blue plastic. To my surprise there is no hall; we get our food literally opposite our cell. Again, I have heard about prison food, and it doesn't come with a good rating. But to be honest, I have seen worse. It's not that bad, it's just the random combinations: I get pizza, new potatoes and cabbage. I would have taken anything, though; I just want to get back in the cell. Tony and I have our food; he has half a loaf of white bread with his dinner. We sit down in the cell; the door gets locked behind us and we watch the news. Now, some people are surprised there are TVs in prison. Trust me, if there weren't, there would be riots twenty-four seven. It is the ONLY thing to do. I only eat the slice of pizza. Tony has the rest and puts it all into sandwiches. He tells me I have a lot to learn.

With your dinner you get a 'Breakfast pack' that contains a couple of tea bags, a couple of sachets of powdered milk, two sugars, and a bag of something that looks like it was collected from the bottom of a rabbit's hutch (muesli) and a small carton of UTH milk, whatever the fuck that is. This was breakfast. Tony makes us a cuppa each with our little kettle. It all feels like we are making happy families with a set of toy utensils and appliances. "Sugar, David? Yes please, Tony." Tony seems quite content; he tells me he is a chef, a trade he learned in Wandsworth when he first came inside twenty years ago. He has been in and out of prison his whole life. I wonder why or how. He seems like a normal guy you would meet down the pub. I am thankful I have been locked in a very small room the size of my bathroom with Tony, and not a nutter.

Lying on our bunks, we are watching the soaps. Tony says I will end up watching them all as there is fuck all else to watch. I don't think Tony knows me well enough yet to know I just wouldn't, so I laugh. I start to fall asleep. I am exhausted, and it has been a bloody long couple of days. Tony asks me if I have a carrier bag. I give him the bag I had my documents in. I do wonder if he is going to use it to kill himself, but he seems OK to me. As I am drifting off, I can hear Tony putting the bag round the toilet pan. I wonder what the fuck he is doing. He proceeds to shit into the bag. There is no divider, no curtain around the toilet; this is right next to my head. Very odd behaviour, but I think maybe it is a courtesy, and he is going to lob his shit out the window or something. After Tony has emptied his bowels, he takes the bag to the sink and he is rummaging through his own shit. I watch Tony start to pick out little balls, that I am guessing have drugs in them. He continues to do this for an hour or so. He has a lot of fucking wraps in a towel. He seems very happy with his haul. I just lie there in amazement and he cracks on, sifting through his shit. Eastenders had nothing on this. Believe it or not I fall asleep with the smell of shit in my nostrils.

I wake in the night to a really sweet smell, a French film on the TV with two birds going down on each other, and some weird noises coming from the bottom bunk. Tony is having a whale of a time wanking away while smoking crack.

I lie there looking at the ceiling, unable to go back to sleep, and wondering where it all went wrong.

I wake early the next morning, not knowing where I am. It takes me a minute to remember I am in prison. Tony is awake. No surprise there, he has been smoking crack all night and probably didn't sleep. Tony is getting ready like he is heading out; he's packing a net bag like he is going on a day trip. I ask him if he is off to the shops. Tony says he is going to speak to the CO (Commanding Officer) to get a job on the hot plate and off E-wing. He says he doesn't need to be acclimatised to prison. I guess he wants to shift the proceeds of the stuff that came out of his arse. I wish him luck. The door opens; Tony is off like a greyhound out of the traps. I stand there and wonder what I am supposed to do… I am in desperate need of a shower, but I need some more time to assess this risk. I peer out of the cell. People are running around doing whatever people do in prison. I don't know what to do; I see an office with a couple of screws in it. I go over and ask about phone credit. They say I will get an induction today, which will answer all the questions I have. I doubt that is true. I have a walk up and down the wing. I am asked for 'Burn' by twenty blokes, which I deduce is tobacco. I head back to my cell.

During lunchtime bang-up, the food is brought to our cells—a baguette in a bag. You know when you buy those baguettes that you put in the oven at home? It's them, but they hadn't bothered to put them in the oven; and a Penguin bar. That makes me laugh: first the kids' cutlery, now kids' chocolate. Anyway, Tony doesn't come back, and I am locked up alone. Then the cell door is unlocked, and a guy walks in, apparently my new padmate. He is young and FULL of energy. Fuck me, he talks 100mph and does not stay still! He tells me his name is Stuart and his life story in three minutes flat and that he has ADHD. He is like a whirlwind. I can't catch a thought. What is he in for…? Well, what I manage to get from the barrage of information is that he assaulted someone. This person was connected and now he is worried someone will get to him inside. He has a ninety-three-page police document he wants me to read to him as he "Doesn't read all that good." I am happy to do this to shut him the fuck up. I can't concentrate as he is asking me a thousand questions. I try to help and give advice but, in the end, I just tell him I don't understand it, which I don't. Stuart is anxious and is pacing the cell, talking to himself. The cell door opens after what feels like a year and I dart out like a greyhound out the traps.

A screw shouts, "INDUCTION" and I am told to go to a room down the end of the wing. I am given a login code when I get there and told to log onto a PC; there are about ten in the room, which is like two cells knocked into one. I wonder if I can ask for a double cell because I might kill Stuart. I log on and it opens a PowerPoint program, which starts with a "Welcome to HMP Wandsworth." The program is designed to tell me all about the prison, the rules and my 'journey'. I click on the first window to get started and the thing just ends and says, "You have completed the induction." There is a lady sat at a table, so I tell her the program crashed and I can't reset it. She tells me I only get one login code. I say I understand that but I never did the induction. She says, "Shut up, you will get your two pounds." What two pounds is she on about? I say I don't need two pounds I need the induction. She gets angry and asks me to leave the room for being disruptive.

Standing outside I wonder if I can get a shower on the sly. But a screw shouts at me and tells me to go to another room below for a Maths and English test. I walk in; a con gives me a piece of paper with questions on it. I struggle through it. The con tells me I scored low, but offers nothing else, so I leave.

Stuart runs up to me and tells me two black guys are staring at him and he is worried he is going to get attacked. I tell him he is being paranoid. After a while I realise he was not being paranoid: they are staring him out, and me too, now! They must think he has recruited me to back him up. Fuck. Stuart says he is going on the 'numbers'. I have no idea what the 'numbers' are, but I think I should probably go on them, too. We get put back in our cells and Stuart is pacing with worry. I am trying to console him, but I am worried too now. Some time later the cell door opens for dinner. Stuart won't leave the cell. I say I will try to get his dinner for him. They laugh at me at the hotplate, calling me a fat bastard when I ask for his meal. You can, however, get a load of bread. I explain the situation to the guy handing it out. He gives me a whole loaf. As I am walking back to the cell, I see Paddy; he sees the loaf of bread and calls me a fat bastard, too. He calls me "Loaf". This nickname stays with me throughout my prison 'journey'. Everyone in prison has a nickname. They are not very witty or clever: Spud, Pikey, Scouse, Brum, Ginger gives a flavour.

Night two is harder than the first night, probably the toughest I had in the whole time I was in.

Stuart won't settle, he is pacing and talking the whole night. I couldn't even watch Corrie.

I miss Tony.

The next morning Stuart is out the cell door very quickly. He realises he will be unlocked before the two black guys further down the landing and he is going to go to the office to go on the numbers. I ask him what the numbers are. He tells me it is a wing for people at risk; I encourage him to do this to get rid of him; I can't go much longer locked in a cell with this guy, I would be up for murder or I would kill myself. I think if he comes back, I will ask to see that nurse who asked if I was suicidal. I wish him luck.

I never see him again.

I have the cell to myself that night. It is a welcome break. I have time to have a good think without distraction—very dangerous. To be honest, at one point I get emotional thinking about my situation and I have a little cry. I pull myself together and I promise myself I won't let the bastards win. I will not show any sign of weakness in here. If I did, I would be a victim very quickly. There and then I decide I am going to put my chest out and hold my head high. I will deal with the situation the best I can and remain strong and determined.

I am spending almost twenty-three hours a day in a cell, because now induction is finished I only get out the cell for about forty-five minutes a day. It takes some getting used to. I still haven't got phone credit, and I am in desperate need of a shower. I am forced to wear the grey prison tracksuit bottoms. I have washed my jeans in the sink with soap, but they are still wet as there is nothing to dry them on overnight. The tracksuit bottoms are ankle swingers, about six inches too short for me. I decide to roll them up into shorts. As I step out on to the landing to head towards the showers a screw sees me and goes spastic at me, as apparently you are not allowed to do this. God knows why. He says I have just done induction, so I know this and it is a show of blatant disregard for the rules. I want to tell him about the computer and my lack of induction, but I don't think he would listen, so I just say, "Calm down, dear." He does not fucking like that! It looks like his head is going to pop off. He shouts that he is going to "Write this up."

What a shit story, I think, why write it down?

I manage to get a shower. Everyone is wearing underwear in the shower, and I do the same, as it seems the done thing. The water is scalding, but I manage to shower without getting raped. I have ten minutes left before bang-up so I start to read the stuff displayed on the walls of the wing. It is the history of the prison. The prison was built in 1851, when it was known as Surrey House of Correction. They used to do hangings at Wandsworth up until 1961 (I wonder if it was for wearing shorts on the wing?). They have had some famous villains in Wandsworth over the years. Most famously, on 8 July 1965, Ronnie Biggs escaped from the prison, where he was serving a thirty-year sentence for his part in the Great Train Robbery. Two years later he fled to Brazil and remained on the run until 2001. I wonder why the prison advertises this. Wandsworth was also home to some other famous cons, like Charles Bronson, and Oscar Wilde.

That day an old boy was put in with me. He was practically mute. I would have been happy spending my whole time inside with him as a cellmate. He didn't care what we watched on the TV and never moaned about anything.

That evening at about nine, a screw looks through the hatch and opens the cell door. In walks a familiar face. Peter. I have known Peter since I was a kid. He is the uncle of one of my friends. I knew Peter was in prison and had been for a long time, but I did not know he was in Wandsworth. Peter says he was told I was in and he wanted to come and see me, to make sure I was OK. He seems to know why I got nicked, I don't know how. He has brought me a pillowcase full of stuff. Noodles, tuna, squash, chocolate, roll-on deodorant, like a prison Santa Claus visiting me. Peter is a really nice guy; I have always liked him. He tells me he is on E-wing to look out for new arrivals, like a Samaritan. This is such a relief. He asks me what wing I would like to go to. I say I would like to go wherever Paddy and Jock went, as they are the only people I know. He says he will sort it, no problem. I say I need to make calls, and he tells me he will make sure I get the two pounds credit tomorrow, which I still haven't got. Peter says he can't really talk now but tells me to come to his cell tomorrow so we can talk properly. I thank him and say I will. My cellmate doesn't move off his bed or ask how or why I got a visit from another con after bang-up. I am glad he doesn't ask, as I don't know either.

Twenty minutes later the same screw comes back again. "Peter tells me you are good stuff." I don't know what to say... he pulls a bit of paper out of his shirt pocket. "Mobile phone £150, Internet phone £300, charger £50, let me know if there is anything else you want, I will give you a price." I nod; he looks at my cellmate and tells him he will 'Finish him' if he talks about this. He walks out and closes the door.

I could do with all of those things to be honest, but I don't know how I would go about paying for it. I never asked.

I have been in a few days now. I still haven't got my anti-depressant medication. I am withdrawing from them and feeling rough: insomnia, dizziness, and the worst vivid nightmares. I speak to one of the screws and ask to go to medical to get a prescription. He tells me I am going to have to wait to get located on another wing. He tells me this will be today or tomorrow, and right enough, later that day I get told to pack as I am moving to C-wing. I thought this was good news, but was it fuck. I get moved to a cell on the threes on C-wing, padded up with a massive Polish guy who only speaks a little English. He's six foot and built like a brick shithouse. Every other word he says is "Kurwa," which is Polish for 'whore/bitch'. He says it so much, it's his nickname.

I didn't know this at the time, but C-wing is for people dependent on substances and/or who have mental health issues; the back half is segregated from the rest of the wing, and this is where the nonces are. C-wing is also for cons that don't work, and we are all locked up twenty-three hours a day. How the fuck did I end up on here?! The wing was fucking wild. People shouting and banging on doors non stop. As soon as I had the chance I was in the office. "I think there has been a terrible mistake." During my nurse assessment she had asked me about drink and drugs. "Yeah, I drink a lot and I love a bit of a nose up," I think was my reply. Then I am on the induction wing asking for my mental health meds. So, they put this all together and put me in with this lot. I can see their thinking to be honest, but I'm not fucking clucking or anything; maybe the 'Calm down, dear' comment had backfired. I protest and ask for a transfer back to E-wing or to be placed on any other wing. They refuse and tell me I will be assessed while on the wing.

I did get my meds though! It was like One Flew Over the Cuckoo's Nest. You had to queue up at a little window at the centre of all the wings to get medication. As you queued up you could see all the way down every wing, I guess it was designed that way so screws could view all the wings from one central viewpoint. I was desperate to get off C-wing. I thought if I could speak to Peter, he might be able to sort it out for me. I was told I might see him on the way out for exercise, as we would pass E-wing. After a couple of days, I spotted him and shouted up to him. I told him where I was, he told me that was bollocks and I shouldn't have gone to C-wing. He told me Paddy and Jock were on B-wing. He said he presumed this was where I went, too. He said he would speak to a CO and try and get me a move.

Back on C-wing, things were OK with Kurwa. He did a lot of press-ups and he ate a lot of protein; all I seemed to eat was rice; my shit was starting to look like sushi. When doing press-ups, Kurwa would say "One–Kurwa, two–Kurwa, three–Kurwa" up to ten. He couldn't count in English past ten so he would just say "Kurwa" for every press-up after that. Funny guy. He was in for ABH; he smashed up someone who broke into his flat, which did not make sense to me. But from what he told me he battered the crap out of the guy. You broke in the wrong flat, mate.

During association, I watch a guy having an argument with a screw. It is heated, and both stand their ground. To be fair to the screw, he could have escalated it and blown his whistle for back-up, but he didn't, and he fronted it out. I thought he managed it well and I thought, maybe the screws were not all cunts, they have a hard job. When we were unlocked the next morning, the guy threw a kettle of boiling shit with sugar in, in the screw's face. He had been planning it all night, shitting and boiling it, waiting for the morning. Why the sugar, you ask? Good question. One I had to ask, too. When sugar is heated it turns into treacle, which melts the skin. Shit in your face is bad enough. This guy was not fucking about. I did feel sorry for the screw. Maybe if he had called in support, they would have wrapped the guy up and he would be down the block, but he decided to deal with it himself and it backfired on him.

While on C-wing I was offered a place on the Drug and Alcohol recovery course. Initially I dismissed it. But the more I thought about it, the more I thought, why not? I knew I was a bit fucked up so why not engage in it and see what happens. I thought it would look good to a judge, too, if I was to apply for bail again or even be convicted and sentenced. The biggest draw to doing it was that I would be moved to a small quiet wing below the C-Cat section of the prison, and after a while on C-wing this sounded great. I told the team, called RAPt (Rehabilitation for Addicted Prisoners Trust), who ran the course, that I was interested.

After a couple of weeks my family and friends had managed to work out the booking system for visits. Prisoners do not book their visits, people on the outside do. You just get a slip under the cell door with the date and time of the visit. Sometimes you don't even get the slip and you have no idea who is visiting. As I was on remand, I was allowed more visits than convicted prisoners. This is pretty much the only benefit of being on remand rather than convicted in prison. My parents visited me first. We had a tough conversation. It was all very British stiff upper lip. Let's not discuss it in detail, everything will be fine, approach. I was desperate to see my sons, but I didn't want them to see me in prison. Which was lucky as security still had to do checks on them for them to be added to my approved visitors list. Better safe then sorry, eh, you can't be letting them dodgy kids with criminal records in, can you?

Visits were hard. I struggled with them at first. You have an hour with loved ones and friends, hearing about what is going on, on the outside, and then back to the desperation of the wing and prison life. I was really down after visits. What was hard was, obviously, everyone who visited me wanted to know how I got myself in this mess. Everyone told me not to talk on the prison phone, write or talk about your case as the screws read the letters. They even listen to the calls and they can record what you are saying on visits. How could I explain to my parents how five kilos of cocaine were found in my flat if I could not talk about it; same with my friends. They had all come to support me and I couldn't explain anything.

They all must have thought I was full of shit, and lying. I could see why. All I said was, I am not guilty, hopefully I will be out soon, and I will explain everything.

I had also now managed to get phone credit. All well and good, but I don't know any phone numbers. Who knows any phone numbers by heart? I had to get them via letter. "Can you send me the phone numbers for...?" Then when you have them, you fill in a form and they need to be vetted by security and approved before you can call anyone. As you can imagine, this takes fucking forever. Anyway, I had managed to add the number for my employer. I call them.

"Hi, it is David. I was arrested and remanded. I had no way of contacting you."

'We know, the police called us to tell us you were arrested, they told us about the drugs and the charge.'

"That was very nice of them, I will find out if that is legal. Where do I stand in terms of my employment?"

'Sorry to tell you, you have been fired. We invited you to attend a meeting or for you to send a representative; it went ahead, and the board decided your employment with us has ended.'

"How did you communicate the invite to this meeting?"

'We sent you a letter.'

"To where?"

'Your home.'

"You knew I was in prison, so you sent a letter to my home inviting me to a meeting. Can you tell me what I was fired for exactly? I am on remand and I intend to fight the charge against me."

'You were fired as you did not turn up for work and have not contacted us.'

"I am in prison. I have had no contact with the outside world until now."

'I am sorry.'

"OK I will get some legal advice on this sacking as I don't feel you have adhered to policy. I believe you have fired me due to the call from the police and the info they shared with you, rather than the stated reason."

On the same day, I received a letter from my landlord to say they were ending my tenancy due to breach of the tenancy agreement. I requested help from a charity in the prison called St. Giles Trust, and that same day they supported me to call my landlord.

"Hi this is David, I received a letter saying you are ending my tenancy, can you tell me why?"

'It is because you were storing and dealing drugs from the property, this is against your tenancy agreement."

"Where have you got this information, this is not correct."

'The police called us, they informed us a large amount of drugs was found in the property.'

"That was very nice of them. I will find out if this is legal. The drugs were not my drugs; I did not give permission for anyone to put drugs in my flat. I am not guilty, and I will be fighting the charges against me. In terms of my tenancy, I have legal advice and I will be taking you to court to stop you ending my tenancy." St. Giles said they would support me to do this. They were the most helpful individuals and service I had met since my arrest. (Actually, the most helpful during my whole prison stay.)

How many people find out they have lost their job and home on the same day?

Chapter 3

B-Wing

"Prisons are built in our hearts and minds. It is only there that we can find the freedom we all deserve."

Sat in my cell with Kurwa playing cards. A screw comes into our cell, tells me he works on B-wing and he's been asked to get me moved there by Peter. He tells me he can arrange this, but I will need to get a job. I said I was up for it; anything to get me out the cell and not banged up twenty-three hours a day. He tells me to pack and he will pick me up after dinner. This is the first time I met Mr B.

Mr B was the best screw I met inside. He was a Spurs fan of all things. You knew where you stood with him; he would tell you to fuck off if he didn't have time, but if he did he would try to help you; if he thought you were being a twat, he would tell you. The cons respected him. Mr B picked me up and took me over to B-wing. He said he was putting me on the twos with a lad who was 'a bit of a dick' but harmless. He tells me the lad is hoping he will get single cell status so might be a bit hostile at first. Great. I was lucky to get onto the twos. Peter must have arranged this for me. The landings are very much like a class system. The ones is Chelsea, the twos Primrose Hill, the threes Shoreditch, and the fours was Peckham. All the reprobates get put on the fours.

Many more people were out on the landings than they were on C-wing, and B-wing was larger, because it didn't have a nonce section. I enter the cell Mr B points out; my new padmate is there even though the doors are open for association. Straight away I can tell he fancies himself a bit. He clearly thinks he is double hard. He is a young mixed-race lad from Birmingham, the worst accent known to man. I tell him I am his new cellmate. He is not happy. He tells me he is on single bang-up. I tell him to go and sort it out with the screws; I just go where I am told to go. Off he pops to see the screws with his bottom lip out like a child. I start to unpack. He comes back after ten minutes with a mate and says, "You better go to that office and tell them you can't be in with me, because I am going to do you as soon as the doors are locked." I tell him that won't be happening, and I will take my chances. Him and his mate stand there, trying to intimidate me, so I make myself a cuppa. I thought about taking a shit, really stamp my authority on the cell, but I didn't want to antagonise him; though I would not be backing down. I go find Paddy and Jock; they are on the twos, as well, I was told. They are with a guy called Steven, in his cell. He was single bang-up; he was in for murder. I had heard about him as he was from my local area. He stabbed someone twenty-six times. Steven invited me into his cell and told me I was solid for keeping my mouth shut. Steven was straight up and asked for my 'Papers'. These are your documents you get with the transcript of your police interviews. I went and got them, and Steven read them. "No comment, No comment, No comment'. I wondered if Steven had asked to see Paddy's and Jock's. I would love to have seen them. Steven welcomed me to B-wing and said if I had any trouble to let him know. I said thanks and said, "Well, funny enough my new cellmate is apparently going to do me after bang-up." Steven got straight up and walked to my cell. I stayed in his. After a couple of minutes, he said it was all sorted and I wouldn't have any issues with my new cellmate. Mr B put his head round the door and called us all queer cunts and it was bang-up so to fuck off back to our own cells. As I walk in, my new cellmate is talking to himself in the mirror and posturing. He says. "I don't like mess, keep it clean and we will be OK" he tells me his name is Calvin. We have an uneasy truce. Calvin is a twat.

The next day I have an appointment at medical. Which I had submitted a request for two weeks earlier. I am taken to a wing out the back of E-wing. Walking back through E-wing it seemed so long ago when I was there. After waiting for two hours for a nurse, I get seen. I explain I have a pacemaker and I was due to have a cardiology appointment in the community, but I was not taken to it; I explain I have had the pacemaker for ten years and it is due a new battery. The nurse looks on the system and tells me nothing has been recorded about the appointment. I tell her I gave the appointment letter, which was sent in by my family, to my officer while on induction. The nurse says she will deal with it. Off I go back to B-wing. It felt like I had had a little day out at the doctors.

It is the lead-up to Christmas but you wouldn't know it in here. This will be my first Christmas away from my family. It is a very depressing thought. A prison Christmas dinner should be interesting.

I am now part of a little crew that go on exercise. There is AJ, Dennis, Pikey, Paddy and Jock. AJ is in for cultivating a massive weed farm, which the police described as "Narnia." Dennis is a pro boxer who got arrested bringing gear into the country via Heathrow airport, and I like them both instantly. Not because of the drugs—they are just top lads. I am not sure why Pikey is in; he is fucking nuts, telling us he is in for something different every day. Today he tells me he is in for jumping off Chelsea Bridge into the Thames for a bet on the way home from the pub. I don't know why he would go to prison for that. We walk round and round in a circle for an hour, mostly taking the piss out of Pikey. It is interesting when out on exercise. Most racial groups stick together. The far right of the yard you have the black lads congregating. On the left you have most of the white lads and in the bottom corner the Polish lads. With a mix in the middle.

As we are walking around, someone shouts "Look at that tranny up in a cell window"; she is flashing her tits to everyone in the yard. Bit of entertainment for the lads. Pikey says he would have a tit wank off her.

This is when I realise everyone uses humour to get through this shithole. We go out every day and just share funny stories we have heard. I look forward to this; it is the only thing to look forward to all day. Pikey: "Did you hear about the two guys fucking each other on C-wing. They are cousins." "Fuck off Pikey, you twat!" is a taste. Pikey is always full of bullshit stories, but Dennis has one today. He asks if we have noticed that fat Tony hasn't been on the wing all day? I had noticed. Tony is the Number One cleaner; he is a Red Band, which means he can move from wing to wing. Dennis tells us Tony was cleaning the Governor's office and he found the Governor's packed lunch that his wife had made him. The story goes that the Governor walked in on Tony eating his packed lunch and he has been nicked for it. Tony is my new hero. I talk to him on the wing and he tells me the story is true and he is back on basic (no privileges) and has been sacked as a cleaner. Top fucking sandwich though, apparently.

On the wing there are some lads who have more teeth than brain cells, and a lot of them don't have many teeth. I am standing on the threes waiting for a shower (better showers on the threes), leaning over the rail having a look about. This lad I have never spoken to stands next to me and seems to want to chat. He looks at me and says, "Do you ever wonder where Christmas trees come from?" I ask him what he means. "You don't see them growing in parks or forests do you?" I say "You stupid bastard, that's because they grow under water. In October divers go down and chop them down, that is why you don't see them." He looks fascinated. So off I go for a shower. When I am finished, I walk down the landing to the stairs at the end of the wing. The lad is telling his mate, who looks just as daft as he is, "Do you know Christmas trees grow under water?!" the other lad says that makes sense, as you don't see them in parks or forests. I am pleased with my day's work.

Speaking of work, I need a job. But I don't fancy all the usual jobs, they look too much like hard work. I've been working since I was fifteen. I need a break. The usual jobs are cleaner, kitchen, stores and kit. I decide I would like to volunteer to work for the St. Giles Trust, helping prisoners keep or get accommodation upon release. I have put in an application, but it is Christmas, so everything is slow.

Things aren't going well with Calvin. We clearly hate each other, and we can't stand each other's company. Most nights I lie on my bunk reading until I fall asleep; Calvin, who has put loads of little mirrors on the wall to make a big one, spends most nights doing some sort of martial arts while looking into his mirror. He loves to talk about the number of birds he has shagged. I am pretty sure he is gay. One night he wakes me up as I am snoring, and I go nuts at him and tell him if he does it again, I will fucking do him. I am not a violent person at all. But don't fuck with my sleep. The next day Mr B grabs me and tells me Calvin has told him I have been threatening him. I tell him he is a top prick and I can't deal with him much longer. Mr B tells me a space is coming up in another cell on the twos and asks if I want to move. I am well up for this. I don't ever want to hear a Birmingham accent again. The next day I move. Calvin and I don't speak, I just pack my stuff and go. I move in with an older Muslim guy everyone calls Uncle. Lovely guy. We have some deep conversations. He tells me about being a Muslim and the Koran; he explains the difference between Sunnis and Shia to me. He prays five times a day. I turn the TV off when he prays and read out of respect. I am not a religious person at all, and I don't believe in any God. To be honest I did not think anyone really was religious any more, but in prison it is massive; everyone seems to be religious, not just to get out their cells on a Sunday for church, actually religious. I did wonder how religious people were on the out. I get along with Uncle and enjoy his company, I learn a lot from him. He is very knowledgeable about world politics. We normally discuss a topic from the news after we eat. I don't know what Uncle was in for and out of respect I never asked.

Uncle was the first person to introduce me to the kettle curry. You can buy loads of ingredients and spices on canteen. Uncle would cook the best tuna curry in the kettle. I was amazed what he could cook in it; he even made a kind of dumpling in the kettle. Gorgeous they were. There was a Korean guy who was in for manufacturing pirate DVDs who would put breadcrumbs on the windowsill of his cell. He would wait for a nice fat pigeon, then grab it and twist its neck to kill it. He would pluck it and boil it in his kettle. You could see feathers coming out of his cell after a catch. The food isn't the best in prison but that is going to extreme lengths. He told me pigeons were a symbol of love and peace in Korea. But he called them "Chickeons." He said Korea had problems with pigeons. He was facing deportation. I thought the quicker they get him home, the quicker the problem would be resolved.

I was starting to feel more comfortable now in Wandsworth. I knew the routine, had some mates, and if I needed something, I avoided all the other screws and went to Mr B. Sometimes he would make me say "Arsenal are shit" to get him to do me a favour, like look up my visits on the NOMIS (National Offender Management Information System) on the prison computer. I started to understand why some people like prison. There are no expectations on you, no rent to pay, no bills, no modern life stresses. Everything is done for you and you are told when and what you can do. I had no idea how long I would be in prison for, but it never scared me like it did when I first arrived. I was lucky, I knew people here, people who had a level of influence and protection. Wandsworth is a distribution prison, though, and I knew if I was sentenced to a longer term, I would be moved to another prison, anywhere in the country, and this protection would be gone.

OK so wanking... I woke up one night; I nearly had a wet dream like a fucking twelve-year-old. I haven't knocked one out since I landed; it's been weeks. They don't put this in the induction. 'How to have a wank when you have no privacy at all.' I had to take the matter into my own hands. I sought out advice. Most people tend to knock one out when their padmate goes on a visit. Uncle doesn't get many as his family are up north. My nuts are like a couple of coconuts, so I need a plan. On the twos I notice a toilet! Every cell has one, so no one uses this toilet. I have a look inside; it is fucking rank. But it has a couple of cubicles. The doors are only about four-foot high but just enough for cover. I go and get a Zoo magazine off Pikey and off I go for a much-needed maintenance wank. Jesus, I redecorated the place. I spent quite a bit of time in that toilet. The screws must have thought I was stashing something in there.

Just before Christmas I received a visit slip. I had no idea who was visiting, no one had said on the phone or letter they were coming, but I went to the visit. To say I was surprised when Kelly walked in would be an understatement. The last time we'd spoken she was in Australia and I had hung up on her when the police walked in. Kelly is fiery, that's what I liked about her, so I genuinely thought she was going to walk up to me and hit me. She didn't; she cried and hugged me. Before I was arrested, Kelly had booked flights to come over and stay with me before flying home to Ireland for Christmas. I felt really bad and apologised and explained I had no way of contacting her. Kelly booking a visit and coming to see me meant a lot. The hour visit flew by very quickly. I tried my best to explain what had happened. Kelly found the whole getting caught wanking by the police very funny, thankfully.

The lads that struggle the most inside are the lads with girlfriends, I think. Lads who are married and are in a committed relationship, they are less worried. But the lads with girlfriends torture themselves, worrying about what their girls are up to while they are locked up. I am thankful for the first time that I am single.

It was nearly time for Uncle to move on from Wandsworth. I would miss him. I was worried about who I would get as a new padmate. I was happy with Uncle. I was sat on a desk on the ones and a guy called Darren said Don wanted to see me. Don intrigued me. He was in cell one on the ones. That is a status in itself. He was always well dressed, in shirt and trousers, and was very polite, and he walked around like he owned the place. Other than that, I knew nothing about him. I asked Darren why Don would want to see me? Darren said he didn't know but it couldn't be good and asked how worried I was? Darren went on to explain that Don was the UK representative of the Italian mafia. I told Darren to fuck off, as this was clearly a wind-up. I walked off to use the phone. A while later Darren came back to me with a magazine. In this magazine was an article about the Italian mafia, with a picture of their UK representative; younger, but clearly the man I knew as Don. My arsehole went, I was shitting myself! I walked down to cell one like it was a walk to the gallows. I had no idea why he would want to see me, what the hell does he want me to do for him? I knocked on Don's cell door; he was sat with another man. He invited me in and offered me a coffee. I declined but thanked him profusely for his hospitality. Don's cell was immaculate, very clean, with a lot of books. Don thanked me for taking the time to come and see him. He apologised for asking Darren to get a message to me. He was very polite! Which made me more worried. Don said he was aware my cellmate was leaving for C-Cat soon. He said Uncle had told him I was a quiet man who was sensible. Don said he had a good friend coming to B-wing soon and he asked if his friend could be my new cellmate. This was a relief as I was worried that he wanted me to do something illegal, which I would struggle to refuse. I told Don I was happy to have his friend as my new cellmate, and I would help him settle in the best I could. Don said he would speak to the screws to arrange it. As I get back to my cell, I realise I am now doing favours for the Italian mafia. I start to worry about who my cellmate will be.

I hear on the prison grapevine that my new cellmate is high up in the Albanian Mafia and someone who is not to be fucked with. I am told he is on E-wing on induction and will be moving over and into my cell in the next few days. I wonder how the fuck I get myself in these situations. My worry is, if he wants to take the piss, and intimidate me, or whatever, I am just going to have to take it. I can't take on the fucking Italian and Albanian mafia!

After a few days, Uncle is packed and ready to move on. I wish him the best and he is full of parting wisdom for me about my future and life. I help him with his bags to the gate at the end of the wing and wave him off.

An hour later, I am introduced to my new cellmate, Albert. He is not what I expected at all. He is very polite too and is a really nice guy! We instantly hit it off. I help him with his bags and to unpack. I just can't link this guy to what I had heard about him and now meeting him. How can this lovely guy be the head of an Albanian crime family, he is so nice! Albert and I get to know each that night. He does not talk about why he is in prison or about his family; he comes across as very humble. He asks me what I am in for but in a 'can I help' kind of way. I wished he could help but I don't know how he could.

As the doors are opened the next morning, we get a lot of visitors to the cell. Loads of Albanian lads are coming down to our cell to pay their respect. They speak in Albanian, so I have no idea what they are saying, but the respect for Albert is very clear. They are almost bowing to him. Albert keeps apologising to me and seems a little embarrassed by the attention. It was like being with royalty; it was funny as fuck. Albert introduces me to his 'best friend'. Tony. Tony is a bloody unit. He looked like he could knock seven shades of shit out of most people. Tony is scary but polite to me too. I do not want to get on the wrong side of Tony. Albert tells me he has anger issues but laughs it off.

My mates are taking the piss out of me telling me Albert and Tony are going to sell my arse to all the other Albanian lads. I am also told Albert is known to order for people's heads to be chopped off who disrespect him. I have no idea if this is true, but I don't want to find out. Over the next few days I hear a lot of scary stories about Albert and his family. But once the door is closed, we get on like a house on fire. Albert tells me he wants to work in the kitchen, but he needs to pass an NVQ on hygiene and his written English is not good enough. I tell Albert to get the books and I will complete them for him, the kitchen will never know. Albert loves this idea and tells me I am a naughty man. I find this funny in the circumstances.

The Albanian lads on the wing now seem to like me, they all say hello and ask if I need anything. One afternoon at lunch I ask Albert if I can have his sachet of soup, as he doesn't like them. Albert gives me his and tells me he will get me some more for all my help. I tell him it isn't necessary, but he insists. The next day I return to my cell just after association. When push open my cell door, I can feel something on the floor behind it. As I look around the door, I see what looks like 200 sachets of soup on the floor. I am so confused. I tell Albert about it. He tells me he told Tony I liked them so now all the Albanian lads are giving me their soups. Albert is laughing his head off; I am too; this is madness. I tell Albert I don't intend to be in prison long enough to finish them all. Over the next few days, I would be sitting in my cell and a load of sachets of soup would come under the door. I knew most of the Albanian lads now, and I told them to stop giving me their soups, but they continued to. I had more bloody soup than Heinz now. My mates are saying I want the soup so I can dip all the bread I get into it. I don't eat much bread, but the nickname 'Loaf' has stuck. Albert asks me why they call me Loaf, and I dread to tell him!

I spend the worst Christmas of my life with Albert and copious amounts of soup. I couldn't even speak to my family on Christmas day, as I couldn't get near a phone. The Christmas dinner was rank. The turkey was thin turkey slices that you would put into a sandwich. I don't know what I was expecting. At least a pig in a blanket or something. The period between Christmas and New Year drags. A lot of the lads have plans for New Year's. They have their orders in. Some have hooch, which is alcohol made from bread, sugar and fruit, usually. Some have paid a screw for some proper alcohol. I hear there is some cocaine about, too. I keep myself away from all that. I just want the New Year to come in. I am due to see my brief at the start of the year. This is all I am focused on. On New Year's Day, Mr B comes to my cell and asks why I haven't got a job yet. I explain I am waiting to get a peer role with the St. Giles Trust. Mr B tells me I have made him look bad as he vouched for me to get on B-wing. I tell him I am happy to do anything until a role with the St. Giles trust comes along. Mr B takes me to an empty cell and tells me he has a job for me. As I look into the cell with trepidation, I see there is a mountain of dirty prison boxer shorts, socks and vests, which touches the celling. It fucking stank! Mr B tells me to sort the whole pile out by separating them into three big trollies. It takes me all day. Happy New Year, David. This is a good representation of how the rest of my year goes.

On January 4th my brief comes to visit me. It isn't the same brief who represented me at court; it is a young Asian woman. She knows next to nothing about my case but tells me I am looking at a six to nine years sentence. I explain to her the circumstance of how the arrest came about, but she does not seem interested in what I have to say. I tell her I am pleading not guilty and she tells me she thinks this is a big risk and advises me to plead guilty.

So maybe this is the time to tell you how I got caught up in this.

I don't really know myself to be honest, but this is the truth.

As you have gathered, I liked a good sniff. My dealer, a good friend of mine, would travel over to me to give me what I had ordered. After a while he suggested he leave a small amount at my flat; that way I could help myself when I wanted it, and he would weigh it and let me know how much I owed him. We did discuss how much was a small amount was. It was never more than a couple of ounces. I showed him where he could leave it in my flat and gave him a key. Whenever I looked in the little hiding place, there was never more than two ounces. It was only ever for personal use. Never had I accepted money to store drugs. This went on for a few months and there was no issue, no large amounts of drugs, he always messaged me to say he was popping round. After a while, I suggested he shouldn't leave any more gear at the flat, as I am sniffing too much because it is on tap. He agreed and that was the end of it. During this time, I had locked myself out of my flat and he came over to let me in with the key I had given him. When we agreed to not leave anything else in my flat, I told him to keep the key in case I locked myself out again. Three months later the police find five kilos of cocaine in my flat. Paddy and Jock, who were my co-defendants, had a further eight kilos. I was in a conspiracy to supply thirteen kilos of cocaine.

I explain this to my brief. I say the police will find nothing on my phone about dealing, they will see I have no money or savings, they will not find another phone that I may have used, and they could not link me to Paddy or Jock.

This is where it is tricky. Yes, I had stored a low amount of cocaine in my flat for personal use. I was never paid to do this. But this had been months previously. I was not arrested for this. I had no idea the five kilos were in my flat, which I was arrested for. As I say, am I innocent? No. Am I guilty of conspiracy to supply thirteen kilos of cocaine? No.

I was taking full responsibility for my actions that led to this and I am willing to take the consequences of these actions. But I am just not guilty of what I was arrested for. I had had no communication with my friend, the dealer, and I would not grass. This may seem the wrong decision to some, but I was brought up to never grass. Never!

I still don't know the full picture of how the drugs got into my flat; my friend said later he did not know either and I believed him. I need to blame myself, and I do. Despite me explaining all this to my brief, she still encourages me to plead guilty. I have no idea what the fuck to do. I am due in court next week to plead.

Chapter 4

Not Guilty

"In the end, everything will be ok. If it is not ok, it is not yet the end."

It is a myth about healthcare in prison. You hear about people getting their teeth fixed and having cosmetic surgery while inside. Utter bollocks. How more people don't die in custody is amazing. Healthcare is shocking. You would hear horror stories of people dying. There was a guy with a fucking brain tumour. They gave him paracetamol. You could hear him crying in pain at night. Cruel bastards. I would say this is not the fault of the clinicians, but of the prison system. People just cannot get unlocked to get to healthcare appointments.

I'd still had no answer regarding getting my pacemaker checked. I submitted a couple of complaints with no real response. During one appointment I did tell the doctor my feet were sore and she said she would refer me to a chiropodist. Great; I will be dead, but I won't have pain in my feet.

One day there is talk there is going to be a big fight on exercise. I have never seen so many people go out for exercise; obviously everyone had heard. You could feel the tension in the atmosphere; some lads were walking like they had a couple of oranges in their armpits. As we got outside, people were just standing around the outside of the yard. There were more screws than usual in and around the little cage they sit in to observe everyone walking round in a circle. After a few minutes, all hell broke loose. The black lads were fighting the Polish lads; one black lad just ran at a group of Polish lads and fly kicked one in the face. It was carnage. I was just stood on the sidelines enjoying the entertainment. There was one lad who had a crutch; he was just swinging it round and round whacking the Polish lads with it. There must have been fifty people fighting. I looked over at the screws; they didn't move, just watched like I was. They just waited for it to settle down and then piled in to split it up. I didn't even see anyone get nicked.

There is this lad I had been chatting to in the showers about football. Some days he says hello back to me and some days he looks at me like I am mad. It turns out they are identical twins, but one is a nutter who sells drugs and one is a quiet lad, who keeps himself to himself. I see them both together on the wing one day, which is a mind fuck. The next day I see one of them and say hi. He tells me the screws have moved his brother to another wing, as they can't tell them apart. I ask him how identical twins end up in prison. He explains to me that he has got his brother arrested. He tells me he was dealing, and he was under surveillance by the police and they found drugs in his flat, which he shares with his brother. As the police also couldn't tell them apart during surveillance, they nicked them both and they both got remanded. I swear I am not making this up!

A peer rep from the RAPt team came to see me about the recovery course I'd applied for. We spoke about the course and what to expect. We had a chat about how much drink and drugs I was using prior to my arrest; we completed a questionnaire and I scored quite high. He felt I needed to do the course. I didn't; I think I am a social drinker and drug user, but I am open to seeing what it's all about and to break the monotony of life on the wing. He tells me it is a twelve-step program. I know quite a lot about this as I have supported clients to AA as part of my job. I am not into all that crap, to be honest, too much like the ten commandments and "Jesus will help you" nonsense for me. But it is less bang-up on a quiet wing and it will look good to a judge, so I tell them to sign me up. The lads call me a lightweight and tell me it is a waste of time, but I have made up my mind.

It is my birthday. Mark who works in the laundry has found a bra. It might be the tranny's. God knows. Anyway, he has nicked it, and dresses up in it and gives me a strip dance, which is very nice of him. Mark is nuts too, if you haven't worked that out. He is the son of a famous snooker player. All he talks about is what he is going to do when he gets out. He plans to arrange for a limo to be at the gate when he is released.

He must have liked dressing up for me because he did it again the next day for the whole wing. He got nicked for it. Obviously, the screws have no sense of humour. It was funny as fuck.

I am due in court. The screws wake you up bloody early, about six. They collect you one by one and take the group down to reception. We are all placed in a big cell with benches down the side and a big glass front so they can watch you. At about seven thirty they load you one by one onto a van to take you to the court you're due to appear in. People are going to courts all over London, Magistrates' and Crown Courts. At least I get to go on a little drive through London. Everyone is a lot quieter than they were on the way to the prison. As we reach the court, I see a screw open one of the sweatboxes just opposite mine, and then he shouts, "Dirty fucking cunt's having a wank!" to the driver. They drag the guy out of his box and ask him who is going to clean up his mess. Obviously, the lad had the same issues I had with finding privacy for a wank and thought, great, "nice little private box to wank in"'. It was like the Amsterdam red light district for the screws looking in the little window at him.

This time I am placed in a little cell in the court alone and not with Paddy and Jock. They take me to see my brief. Again, someone I haven't met before: a young lady, who has "read my notes". Good start. She advises me to plead guilty. I ask her if I should plead guilty if I am not guilty. This question seems to throw her, and she says I am not thinking about the consequences of a guilty verdict. I say I am considering the consequences of going to prison for something I do not think I should be going to prison for.

We only had ten minutes together before we were ushered to appear. Again, same charade as before: stand and say your name. I pleaded 'Not Guilty' and my bail was denied again. I was asked if I wanted to see my brief after. I didn't see the point, to be honest. I told them to book a visit and for the brief to come and see me at Wandsworth. I did see her briefly, however, and she told me the CPS would be considering my plea and that they would inform us of their decision on whether to proceed to trial or not.

On the way back to Wanno in the sweatbox, I am dejected again. I feel the system is flawed and nobody gives a shit if I go to prison for ten years. The police have a narrative and haven't bothered to investigate anything as far as I can tell; they have three people in custody. The various briefs don't give a shit and God forbid I try to defend myself at a trial. I don't know what I expected really. I think I expected the police to investigate my involvement, and, if they could not find any evidence for it, drop the charge of conspiracy. I expected a brief, just one, not a series of them who didn't communicate with each other. Just one brief who knew my case and would advocate for me and fight for my freedom. Maybe I had watched too many TV shows. I can't watch any of them now, knowing they are all bullshit.

Despite all this I still hold hope, hope that the CPS will not want to have a costly, lengthy trial. Hope that in a few weeks I will know my fate and it will be in my favour. I hold hope that I can satisfy a jury that I had no knowledge of this conspiracy to supply thirteen kilos of cocaine. I mean, come on! My brain can't even fathom this; how would a jury believe I was guilty? I have no money, no personal property of any value; I have a modest lifestyle—I hadn't had a holiday in years; I work full time. I don't have a car. Does this sound like someone involved in drug dealing on this scale? This was my hope now, that I could fight for my freedom and get a 'not guilty' verdict from a panel of twelve of my peers.

Chapter 5

Rehab

"Better to lose count while naming your blessings, than to lose your blessings by counting your troubles."

My time had come to start the rehab course with RAPt. I pack my stuff. Albert doesn't want me to go but he understands, and he wishes me well. I will miss him, believe it or not; I liked his company. He is my friend, and he is part of the Albanian mafia. It is impossible to make friends in prison, due to the transient nature of the life: you can be moved so often, from one wing to another, or transferred to another prison. As Wanno is a disbursement prison, people go as quickly as they arrive. It is weird, because you have a kind of moral dilemma in your head: do you want to make friends with someone who could be anything—a murderer, or a rapist? I speak to people every day and I have no idea why they are in prison. But equally, do you want to isolate yourself, and judge people? I am in here. How can I judge someone else?

The RAPt course is six-week's long. Two group sessions a day Monday to Friday and a once weekly one-to-one with your session support worker. There is an expectation you will attend other activities also. I haven't worked out what they are yet. I am collected and taken over the C-Cat part of the prison. Walking around the prison grounds, there is rubbish and rotting food everywhere, which people have thrown from their cell windows. No wonder there are so many rats. People talk about the massive size of the rats at Wanno; I took it with a pinch of salt, until I saw one in the yard, out of my cell window. It was the size of a small dog. At least they can't get into the cells, being so big.

The RAPt unit is under K-Wing. As we walk in, I see the RAPt wing is smaller than all the other wings I have been on and is much quieter. There is a lot more literature on the walls, but it is all about recovery. This is going to be a long six weeks, I think. I meet the facilitator and my support worker. He is an American guy called Brad. I knew then it would be a bloody long six weeks! He welcomed me and showed me to my new cell. Once you have been in one cell, you have been in them all. This one was the same as all the rest of them. The RAPt wing was in the basement, though, so there was very little natural light in the cells down there. I am introduced to my new cellmate, Mick. Mick is in his forties and he looks tired. He is quiet, but he seems agitated. We are told we will be unlocked for an afternoon group session after lunch, which is brought to the cell. Still the same horrible baguette as every other day. Mick tells me he does not give a shit about the course and that he is doing it to please other people. I tell him I am much the same: I am open to change but I'm not having any preaching or God bollocks.

I was having it whether I liked it or not. We were taken to a room, well, two cells knocked into one again. We sat in a circle. We were told about the course and the twelve steps (ten commandments). We were told the AA Serenity prayer.

"God, grant me the serenity to accept the things I cannot change, the Courage to change the things I can, And the wisdom to know the difference."

We are told we will all quote this at the end of the session. No fucking way I am praying. I was straight in.

'I'm not praying. I was told this was not religious based.'

"It is not a prayer."

'It starts with GOD.'

"It can mean your higher power."

'What's that when it is at home?'

"It is someone greater than yourself."

'Dennis Bergkamp is the only man greater than I am.'

"Use him then."

'Dennis Bergkamp grant me the serenity...'

Good start to the course. I can see I have upset the facilitator; I have compared his God to a footballer. (I never see any God do what I have seen DB do.)

Next he asks us to introduce ourselves, say why we are here. Some lads start "My name is_____ and I am an alcoholic."

It gets to me.

'I am Dave and I like drink and drugs too much.'

I am asked if I am not ready to admit I have an addiction. I challenge this and say I don't have an addiction. I just like drink and drugs.

The rest of the session I am just listening to the others. Some are clearly there to try to change. I think I am ready to change, but not the way they want me to. At the end of the session the facilitator asks to speak to me. I was expecting this. He asks me not to be disruptive in the group. I say that is not a problem, if I don't need to pray or admit to something I am not. We get into a long dialogue about it not being a religious group. I highlight the God bit and the pray bit and the power higher than me bits. We don't agree and he asks me just to listen for the first few sessions. I can do that. I listen to bollocks every day. I can tell this isn't the end of the conversation. I know this makes me sound like a dick, but I was warned about being radicalised in jail. Seriously though. Why the religious element? It's not needed. As I get back to my cell Mick says, "What a load of old bollocks."

The next day was much the same, and the day after that and the day after that. I would not say I was an alcoholic and I would not chant a prayer at the end. I just sat quietly. There was this one session about a time when we have lost control due to drink or drug use. Now this should be fun, I thought! We went around the room and most had pretty boring stories to be honest. I had too fucking many and told a shit one. It was like a stand-up routine for me. "You will fucking love this one!" I was asked to not glorify the story, which pissed on my parade. Anyway, we get to Derrick. I've not heard Derrick say a word since we have been there. Yep, I like him. Derrick tries to pass but Brad presses him and tells him he needs to start sharing. Derrick goes quiet, then leans forward and says, "Well, me and my mate, right," and I knew this was going to be good. I sit forward.

"Me and my mate Pat were pissed as fuck, walking in Surrey somewhere. We came across a horse in a field. I bet Pat he couldn't jump on it. Pat got on but the horse bucked, and he got thrown off. Pat then bet me I couldn't get on it. He holds my beer and I got on it no problem, and I rode it round the field like I was the Lone Ranger. Then Pat gets on the back of the horse, too, so we decided we liked the horse and we wanted to take him home. Anyway, twenty minutes later me and Pat are riding the horse on the hard shoulder of the motorway. We heard some sirens, so we diverted off into a field. After a while we came across a little housing estate. We could still hear the sirens, so we hide the horse in a big bin shed. The police caught up with us and found the horse. We got nicked and the next morning we were in court on rambling charges! The judge said it was the first case of rambling in 100 years."

I am laughing my tits off; I think it is the best story I have ever heard. I look round the room and everyone is shaking their heads at the story. Brad asks how the story makes Derrick feel? Derrick just shrugs. I thank Derrick and say it is the best story I have ever heard. Brad asks me not to glorify the story. I don't think it needed me to; it's a great fucking story.

One morning I am told it is a yoga class and I laugh out loud. I thought it was a joke! It wasn't. A bunch of cons doing yoga to stop them getting fucked up. I'd heard it all now. When the doors were opened, I hid behind the door. I knew the yoga teacher wouldn't know how many should be in the class. I got away with this for a few sessions, then a screw caught on that I was not there. He took me to the facilitators and wanted me thrown off the course. I reminded them it was an 'expectation' to attend other groups, not a requirement. I was told I could stay (I didn't ask to) but I needed to change my attitude. My support worker Brad and I had a one to one that afternoon. He got all psychological on me, analysing me from the books he had read. He tried a bit of reverse psychology on me, bless him, and said I was scared to change. Straight out of a 'how to motivate someone' manual. He was right, though, I was scared. Scared I would just be a bum now, an ex-con who fucked it all up and is now a pisshead.

Once I realised I was scared and I admitted it to myself, I started sharing in group; I opened up. I did want to look inside myself and see what was there, but I was scared of what I might find, and that I might not like it. We started to talk about feelings in group. I had no idea what they were on about. 'Feelings? I'm a geezer! I don't have feelings!" I really struggled, not only to share my feelings, but also to identify and articulate them. Brad asked me to write a diary every day about how I was feeling. At first it was impossible for me, so Brad suggested I started with sad faces and happy faces, as I couldn't use words. I was like an illiterate with my feelings. I had never done it; I had never asked myself how I felt. With practice I was able to articulate how I felt and why I thought I felt that way. It was probably the hardest thing I have ever done. My depression and anxiety got worse. I was having nightmares, panic attacks, insomnia and shakes, but I knew it was a positive thing to do. I started to crave drink and drugs. Brad told me I was having a 'dry relapse', a term I didn't understand at the time. One weekend during this period was my worst inside. It was Easter weekend; we were locked away on the Thursday evening and the door never opened again until the Tuesday morning. It was like being a caged animal. Imagine being in a twelve-by-eight room with another person for about 100 hours. My cellmate actually started head-butting the wall and I had to press the panic bell for him on the Monday evening; it took them two hours to answer.

I started to enjoy group. I still didn't say I was an alcoholic or chant the mantra, but I felt part of a group and I wanted to try to help the other lads and not be a dick. I started to respect Brad and listen to what he had to say. The guy was an American working in a British Prison. I knew there was more to him, and I asked him. Brad said he was indeed in recovery himself. He'd come to the UK to start a new life. He now had a British wife and kid and wanted to support others. I began to try to spend more time with Brad, sought time with him. I played devil's advocate with him and we had some good chats. He started to listen to what I had to say—I think. I started to talk about alternative methods to group work and working with people who were dependent on substances. I spoke about my job, the one I no longer had. One that I loved. Brad listened and challenged me and my beliefs about change and alternatives to twelve-step programs. I like that. I like when someone tells me I am wrong. If someone tells me I am wrong, I want to know more, I want to listen and challenge them and my own belief. I told Brad I did not identify as an alcoholic, as many of the clients I worked with were dependent on alcohol. They would spend every penny they had on alcohol; they would seek it first thing in the morning and if they did not manage to obtain any, they would fit and could die. I said I did not relate to this. Brad said he felt I was more of a functioning alcoholic, and he said he did not think I could get over it unless I could have ownership of it and admit I had a problem. I agreed alcohol probably was a problem for me, but 'alcoholic' is such a strong term of reference. I felt it was too much of a pigeonhole statement to brand anyone who drank too much an alcoholic. How can I have ownership over something I don't identify as? Why the need to label and diagnose everything?

While on the course I had another legal visit. Once again, it was someone I had never met before, but who was at least clued up on my case. She wanted to listen to me, too. I told her I would not be pleading guilty to 'Conspiracy'. There was no way. By the time I appeared in court, I would have been on remand for six months. I told the brief I would plead guilty to a lesser charge. I would not plead guilty to supply, only to possession. My brief told me she had put this to the CPS and they had not accepted it. I didn't understand what they thought they had on me, other than five kilos of cocaine, that is; I knew I was not involved. I told my brief that if they would not drop the conspiracy charge, I would be willing to go to trial. It would be a massive risk. I could get ten years if found guilty. The court system is flawed. It is set up to make you plead guilty whether you are or not, because the consequences of a guilty verdict after a trial are so huge. My brief told me I might need to have a 'Newton Trial', which is a trial within a trial. When the defence and the prosecution cannot agree on a charge, you go in front of a judge and he decides. My brief warned me against this and said only ten percent of cases are successful and if you lose, you lose your credit (reduced time). Again, it seemed the system was flawed. My brief said it was a game of cat and mouse on the day in court. This really annoyed me, as this was my life. This wasn't a game for briefs to play. We spoke about possible sentences. Found guilty at trial, I was looking at ten to twelve years. Guilty plea: four to five years for my role. If I got a lesser charge, maybe possession with a role as a custodian of drugs, maybe three years. This is including any credit for good character and first arrest. At this point I would have taken three years. Under four years I could get out on a tag for the last six months. I told my brief I would plead guilty to possession, with the hope of a three-year sentence, but I would go to trial if they wanted to proceed with the conspiracy charge. She said she would see me in court in a few weeks.

A couple of weeks later I completed the RAPt course. It is the first thing I have ever graduated from. I got a lot from it. I felt stronger and clearer. Brad encouraged the group to go on and be peers for the RAPt service while in the prison system, but pointed at me and said, "Except for him and his clear disdain for God and the twelve steps." Brad shook my hand and told me I was a pain in his arse, but he would miss me. The group got in a huddle and for the last time chanted the serenity prayer. This time I shouted it, and everyone cheered. I felt I owed Brad and the group that. I am still not a fucking alcoholic though.

Chapter 6

Fate

"Once you choose hope, anything is possible."

Like six weeks previously but in reverse, I was collected by a screw and escorted back to B-Wing. I made sure this was where I was going back to this time, so they didn't dump me on C-Wing again. Before we left, we were given one last motivational speech about remaining clean and dry and not succumbing to temptation. When I got back on the wing, nothing had changed; it was still very loud, with people walking around looking busy. Mark was like he was on speed, mad excited as he was being released in a few days. Mr B was not around; I was told I would be on the threes. Not good. I wanted a cell back on the twos, but there were none available. I walked down the wing and found my new cell. No one was in there, but the door was open. I went in and the cell was a mess. There was porn all over the walls, (not a problem at all) and there was Polish writing everywhere. It was more like a crack den. There was a sheet half hanging across the window and crap everywhere. I wanted to go to the landing office and ask the screws if I could have another cell, but I decided to wait until Mr B was back on and ask him. So, I started to unpack my stuff and tidy up. When the door was opened for association, I got to see some of the lads and catch up on what'd been going on. Nothing much it turned out. I grabbed a shower and went back to the cell; I still hadn't met my new cellmate. Couple of hours later and he still wasn't banged up with me. One of the screws coming around to do the evening count opened the door and asked me where he was; I said I had no idea, and told him I hadn't even met him. An hour later he came back and asked me again. Again, I said I had no idea where he was. I told him the cell was a mess when I got here, and I wasn't even sure if I had a cellmate, as there wasn't any personal stuff at all. He told me there should have been a "Mad little Polish lad" in with me. He never did come back that night, and the screws had no idea where he was; they kept checking, and then just stopped. The last screw I saw that night through the door just shrugged and said, "Fuck knows where he is."

For two days it was just me and the girls on the wall in that cell, and it was as close to bliss as I had come since being arrested. Peace and quiet. But after two days, I came back to the cell after association and there was a slim, short guy standing in my cell looking pissed off. He couldn't speak English and was going fucking nuts. He wanted to fight me. I didn't know what the fuck was going on, but I guessed it was my missing cellmate! As he came at me, I just picked him up like a child and put him outside onto the landing to calm down. After a few minutes he came back with someone. I wasn't getting caught trapped in the cell with two lads coming at me, so I stayed on the landing ready to have it out with a couple of mad Polish lads. But his mate spoke to me in English, and he was calm. He asked me where his friend's stuff was? I told him I had moved into the cell two days ago and when I did, there was nothing in the cell except rubbish. He translated back to his little friend who was still raging. The guy told me the little guy was nicked and taken to the block, and that when he was taken he'd had loads of stuff in the cell. I told him that when I got there the cell door was open, and that it must have been ransacked and all his stuff taken. I was not sure they believed me but off they went down to the screws' office to complain. While they were gone, I put a little package of stuff together for the lad. I felt sorry for him. Some tea, coffee and milk. Few bits from the canteen and some decent prison clothes I had managed to get my hands on by giving someone in the stores a bit of burn to sort me out some of the better clothes. When he came back he was angry, but apologised via his friend. He told me his name was Januz and thanked me for the package I had given him. I asked his mate what he had done to go to the block. He told me he had made a lot of hooch, which the screws found wrapped around the pipes in the cell (to warm up and ferment). Not enough to go to the block for. Just a nicking. But his friend told me Januz was crazy and drunk, so he bit a screw on the face. None of this was shocking to me now. This was daily prison shit. But what did shock me was that I had just completed six weeks of rehab and when we left, we were told to avoid temptation. The screws had then decided to place me in a cell with a known brewer of hooch. I mean, what chance did you have in there!?

The next morning, Mark was due for release. I wanted to go and shake his hand and wish him well. I expected to find him bouncing off the walls, but when I got to his cell, he seemed sombre to me. There were a few lads there, so I didn't ask him if he was OK. But I wished the mad bastard well and off he went. Later that day, some lads who were going to court and were in reception when Mark was being discharged told us he was crying because he did not want to leave! I couldn't get my head around it. Why the fuck would anyone want to be in this shithole?! A lot of lads were laughing about it, but I felt sorry for him. How can you be that institutionalised you'd rather be in prison than a free man? Apparently, he said he had nothing to go out to; he said he had his friends in Wanno, and was well-liked.

Now I was back on B-wing, I needed a job. And not a job sorting out shit-stained pants! I managed to speak to the St. Giles Trust, and they invited me down to their offices under C-wing for an interview to be a peer. I was interviewed by one of the team and another peer; I thought that was great, upskilling someone. I explained my role prior to my arrest and my experience in the homeless sector. I had a lot of knowledge of housing providers and housing law and I thought I could be a real benefit to the team. They took me on as a peer there and then. My role was to come down to the offices in the morning, and collect referral sheets that had been completed by cons. I would then go onto my wing and interview them about their housing needs, completing another section of the form. I would then give the completed forms back to the St. Giles team and they would action as needed, whether it was to support someone to keep their tenancy or to source accommodation post-release. I would also deliver movement slips to anyone the team needed to see to get them down to their offices. I was given a purple jumper and T-shirt to wear, with the St. Giles logo on. Some of the lads took the piss, but I loved it. It gave me purpose. I am much better in myself when I am helping others. That is when I am happiest, when I am thinking of others and not myself.

My court appearance was fast approaching. I had another legal visit. My brief told me the CPS had disclosed some more evidence that they previously hadn't shared. The CPS informed my brief that they did not accept my basis of plea as my fingerprints were found on one of the kilos of cocaine, so I must have known it was there. I told my brief this was a

lie, impossible. I swore on the lives of my children. And then it hit me...
the big copper in my kitchen thrusting a kilo at me, after the other one
had asked if he had 'Done it yet'. I felt utterly defeated. I was fighting bent
coppers now, too, who had made sure they would get a conviction. At
that point, I gave up. I said I would plead guilty to 'possession with intent
to supply Class A drugs' if the CPS would accept that charge. My brief
spoke to them and came back to me to say they had accepted but they
needed a basis of plea statement. Basically, a statement saying that I was
guilty and what I was guilty of. My barrister and I wrote a one-sentence
plea and I signed it at another legal visit. I was told a couple of weeks later
that there was a problem. I was in phone contact with my barrister almost
daily now, and one day she said the CPS had not accepted my basis of plea
and they wanted more in the statement. I couldn't believe it. They
accepted me saying I was guilty, and they wanted me to fabricate a story
to go with it. I had no idea what to say. I was pleading guilty, even though
I wasn't, and they knew it; they had the evidence, or lack of. I told my
barrister I refused to collude with the CPS and they just had to accept
what I had signed. What is the difference, I would plead guilty? I stood my
ground on this for a while, but so did the CPS. I gave up again. I wrote a
basis of plea that said I was paid to store drugs in my flat by a third party.
And that I had complete knowledge they were there. This was submitted
to the CPS and again they refused it: they said they wanted a figure, how
much I was paid to store the drugs. I felt I was being humiliated. Is sending
a person to prison not enough for these people? I didn't have a clue how
much someone would be paid to do this. I guessed and said I was paid
£300.

Two weeks later. Being taken to Southwark crown court; we were late
due to traffic and getting everyone on the van. This time I was taken
straight up to the courtroom. I stood in a glass box looking across the
court at the police and CPS. I had been dragged through a system I did not
understand, which made me feel worthless. I felt no one had listened or
cared. I bowed my head and pleaded guilty to the court. I was given a
date when I would appear to be sentenced and taken back down to the
cells. I was taken to see my brief again. She asked me to get as many
character references as possible, as this would help when it came to

sentencing; I asked her how long a sentence to expect. She told me four years was likely.

The next few weeks were hell. I was angry at myself, at the police, and the CPS. I was angry with my representation, and with the court system. I was just angry. Being angry in prison is not good. I became introverted for a while. I didn't want to speak to anyone, inside prison or out; I just wanted to be left alone. This period is bit of a blur. I just remember being angry and arguing with screws, mostly. I think I sought confrontation with them to release some anger. I had no other avenue to get my frustration out. I was placed on basic for calling a screw a cunt. That just made me angrier.

Very soon I was back to court, this time with Jock and Paddy; they were nervous, I could tell. I was too, but I felt so low and had so much disdain for the court I thought I didn't care what happened. I had written a letter to the judge about being sorry and all that crap. I had a suit sent to the prison and was wearing it for appearance's sake. A lot of friends and colleagues had written character references for me, which I felt I did not deserve. Jock said he would be happy with eight years. Paddy said he would be happy with nine, as he had a previous conviction and another charge. I said I hoped for less than four years. When I walked into the courtroom, I looked across and saw so many family and friends there. I had so many emotions, I couldn't even settle on one. I felt loved, but felt I had let them all down. I couldn't look at them. Each of our barristers went through statements about us individually and the judge listened. He would now hand down our sentences. He started with Paddy, who had more charges than Jock and me. The judge gave him six and half years! My heart rate shot up and suddenly I had hope. He got three years less than he expected. He then went on to Jock. He gave him six and a half years! I think a smile came across my face, fuck me, if that is what they got on a conspiracy charge with previous and another charge, I must be getting two to three years! The judge got to me; I was feeling positive. The judge said it was clear I was of good character from the references he had received, which was many. But he pointed out how I had let them all down. He then brought up my basis of plea and said he did not believe I was paid £300 to store such a large quantity of drugs. He said I had lied on my basis of plea. He was right; I had made that up as I was forced to fabricate a story. I had no idea where he was going with this; he hadn't said anything negative about my co-defendants. The judge looked down his glasses and sentenced me to five and a half years in prison. I was gob smacked. How the fuck had he got to that sentence?! I was told I was looking at four years! I wanted to go nuts and scream at the court. He must have made a mistake. I didn't know what to do. As he was summing up, I took my tie off as a sign of my disdain. I wanted everyone to know I had no respect for the judge, or the court, and that I did not agree with the sentence. That is the best I could do. How British: I am ready to kill someone, but I take my tie off in anger.

Five and a half years.

Five and a half years.

Five and a fucking half years?!

To compound my misery, Jock and Paddy were celebrating, jumping up and down in joy. They received much shorter sentences than they'd expected. They didn't say a word to me. Nothing. At this point you would think nothing would really surprise me. I was in utter shock. I was past angry; I just couldn't comprehend the decision or how I could do that length of a sentence. I had served six months already and it was hell on earth. Even with early release on licence, I might have to do another three years. How could I do three more years? My brief wanted to see me. I refused. I just couldn't see her. She saw my family and friends, who challenged her and the work her firm had done. She said the sentence was harsh and I could appeal the decision.

In the sweatbox on the way back to Wanno, now knowing my fate, the harsh reality of a long sentence, I was a broken man. From the small window in the prison van, I saw my friends and family standing outside the court; they also looked upset. What had I done to my family? I instantly regretted pleading guilty. I should have gone to trial and fought for my freedom. I felt like a coward. Like pleading guilty was the easy way out. I was so sombre on the way back to Wanno, but right then, at the lowest I have ever been, I decided I would not be a victim. I would not let this define me, or my life. I had lost everything, but I was going to get it all back. I was going to do everything I could to make the time serve me. I would better myself and, as much as possible, be positive, and take on every situation with purpose. I saw this as the end of one part of my life, and the start of the next. As the big gates opened to the prison, I realised I was not angry now. I was determined. Fuck them. Fuck them all.

Chapter 7

C-Cat

"Don't wait for the storm to pass - learn to dance in the rain."

In the end it turned out I had nearly two years, three months more to serve at Her Majesty's pleasure. I could spend it feeling sorry for myself, and being angry at the world, or I could use it to try to better myself and to work on myself. I needed to forgive myself first. I had been an absolute idiot. I can, and do, only blame myself for the mess I was in. I told myself everyone makes mistakes; some are bigger than others. Mine was a pretty fucking big one, which had now led me to lose nearly three years of my life. I had to let go of any anger. Yes, the system is broken. But I put myself in that system. I had to get this right, or the resentment and anger would destroy me. I felt focused. I knew what I wanted to do and knew what I needed to do to achieve it. I wanted to educate myself. I left school before I completed any exams, and I wanted to get some qualifications. I wanted to get fit. I needed to lose weight. I had lost quite a lot already, but I wanted to be fit. I needed to work toward my release and what I would need when I was released. Going to prison is one thing; being recalled to prison, post-release, is another. Half of Wanno seemed to be people recalled while on licence. I had lost my home and I needed to start a plan, so I would not be released homeless. The stats on people leaving prison homeless are shocking. I needed to be employable upon release. I desperately wanted to continue to work with the homeless. It is my vocation. But achieving this with a conviction of intent to supply Class A drugs would be hard.

First, I signed up to gain an NVQ Level 3 on a course the St. Giles Trust ran called 'Advice and Guidance'. This would give me a qualification and it would be good training if I planned to get back into the homeless sector. It was too late for me to start education in Wanno, as I would likely be dispersed soon to another prison because I had now been convicted. I started training; I went to the gym as much as I could. I had no chance of getting near the weights, so I just did CV training like running and rowing. I wanted to get some self-education books, especially to try to improve my English. But Chris Grayling the prisons Minister had banned books being sent in. He said the screws did not have time to go through all the parcels for security checks. Education is the best way to reform and empower prisoners, but how do you do that without books? There was a library in the prison. How the fuck you got there was anyone's guess. I saw a poster that said a screw picked people up on the twos on a Tuesday during association and escorted them to the library. I waited one night like an idiot for half an hour, and when I asked a screw if he could take me, he actually laughed at me. I asked to go to the library constantly. When Mr B got tired of me asking he took me up to a library above the visits hall. It wasn't a great library, but I got out as many books as I was allowed, which was five. I took out two educational books and three novels. When I got back with my books in my arms, the looks I got you would have thought I'd just walked on the wing with a bunch of flowers and balloons.

My young Polish cellmate was doing my nut in; I told him I needed to find a new cellmate, so his friend said he would swap with me and told me he was in with an old guy who was quiet. I was well up for some quiet. I went and introduced myself to his cellmate; his name was John. He seemed nice so I agreed to move. Mr B sorted it out for me. Yep, you guessed it, out of the frying pan and into the fire; as soon as we were behind the door, John was like Alf Garnett; he was the most racist person I have ever met. Vile man. He had written EDL all over the cell and would not stop saying 'Them blacks' and 'Fucking Muslims'. I wasn't having it, so first night behind the door I told him I would give him a dig if he carried on. He continued but did the "Oh, sorry, I forgot you like them" crap. I was worried someone would come into my cell, see the EDL graffiti and think it was me, so I had to cover them all up, with page three girls mostly. I did meet a guy everyone called Snakes through him, though. John sold his medication to Snakes. Snakes was fucking mental, as most people seemed to be in Wanno. His nickname came from the fact he had a slit in his tongue, so it looked like a snake's tongue. I asked him if it was a birth defect, he said he'd had it cut because the birds loved it around their fuck button. I am all for doing something to pleasure a bird, but I am not cutting my tongue in half. He also showed me a tattoo of a bumblebee on his cock. Why would he get that tattoo, you may ask? He said, because it stings when he pisses. Fucking loon. Naturally, I looked forward to Snakes coming to my cell. I was fascinated by him. One night I came back to my cell and Snakes was sat on a chair watching the TV. I asked him where John was and Snakes said, "I put him under the bunk, he was being racist. So I have put him under there to teach him a lesson." I looked under the bunk and there was John curled up. I called him a prick and Snakes and I had a cup of tea and watched Homes Under the Hammer.

I hadn't had any visitors for a couple of weeks. Friends and family all said they had been trying to call to book visits but not getting any answer from the visits office. One of the cons who worked on reception told me the screws rotate roles within the prison, and the lady who booked the visits the past two weeks was deaf! Equality gone mad. The lads made a lot of complaints, but they fell on deaf ears. (Sorry, pun intended.)

A screw came in my cell for checks and saw my page three girls on the walls. It is against policy, apparently, to have them up, as the female screws might get offended. He told me I had to take them down. I explained I had put them up to cover John's EDL slogans. I told him I didn't fancy someone seeing them and thinking I was a racist. The screw agreed.

He came back ten minutes later with a black marker pen and he used it to obscure all the nipples and fannies of the girls. It was equally hilarious and heart breaking. My new game was to replace them all with new girls to keep him on his toes.

My solicitor contacted me and offered to appeal my sentence. Obviously, I wanted to appeal and try to reduce my sentence, but on the other hand, I just wanted to get on with it, I was done with courts, judges and solicitors. I was told the judge could not add any more time if I was unsuccessful, and so, after speaking with my family, I decided to appeal. I wasn't going to hold my breath, but I had nothing to lose.

I was ordered to appear in court again on a 'Confiscation Order' as part of the Proceeds of Crime Act. Basically, the court would look at my finances for the last six years and then decide if any finances were gained from crime. This was quite funny to me; I was broke. I was about five thousand in debt. The crazy thing is, if the judge believes you did get earnings from crime but you do not have the funds to pay it back, they can add to your sentence and even take future earnings. I woke up to a flashlight in my face at 6am. I had no idea I was going to court that day. In the holding cells I was chatting to an Arab lad who was also going to court. When we arrived there were loads of paparazzi jumping up taking pictures through our van window. They did not know who was in which window, so they we were taking pictures through all of them while the van was waiting outside the court. They took so many of me I was bloody blinded. I knew someone on the van was high profile. I was told in the cells that the Arab guy I was talking to had attacked three women with a hammer in a hotel in London. I had seen it on the news, but I didn't know it was him. He got life in prison. Despite me sacking my brief after my sentencing, she was back again. She told me she'd been at the court the previous day expecting me. She had the wrong day. As we sat down in a room to discuss my financial history she opened her laptop and looked confused. She explained to me she had brought her husband's laptop by mistake. She didn't have my case notes. I didn't even respond; I expected this shit now. I told her I would not be paying anything to the court, not only because I had no money, but also because I had never made any money from criminality. In court, the judge ordered me to pay one pound. Watching my brief explain to the judge that I would not be paying one pound was funny. The judge looked through loads of books and said I must serve one extra day in prison if I did not pay. I informed the court I would do the extra day. I knew it would be a pain in the arse for everyone, the judge, my brief and the prison, as all my paperwork would need to be changed. I sat there with a little smile on my face. This was my way of putting my finger up at them all.

It was time for me to move again. With my luck, I was worried my next cellmate might be Charles Bronson. I had been re-categorised from a B-Cat prisoner to a C-Cat, which has less security and fewer restrictions. I was to move over to K-wing above where I did the RAPt course. I was taken over and I was given a cell on the threes, right at the end of the landing next to the wing library. I was chuffed about that. I never had the chance to take my other books back to the main library in the B-Cat. I wondered if they would add time to my sentence for this. It seems they use any excuse. I was happy to go onto K-wing; it was where most of my mates were. The C-Cat part of the prison had three wings in all. The other two were G-wing, which was crazy, and H-wing, where the white-collar club were; I didn't trust any of them, so K-wing was my new home. I couldn't see any difference from the B-Cat part of the prison at all to be honest.

My new cellmate was a scouser named Frank. Frank was in for murdering his wife. He was adamant from minute one to me that he was innocent. I could tell he wasn't. He would protest how the evidence against him was misleading, but then hint that he could have killed her if he'd wanted to and get away with it; he was constantly contradicting himself. It was clear he had a Personality Disorder. He had been convicted by a court of her murder and sentenced to life. He told the police he was in Germany at the time of the murder. Pretty easy to prove one way or the other. After he bumped her off, he stole her jewellery and was seen on CCTV trying to sell it on the same day of the murder in a pawnshop in Wrexham. What a thick bastard.

I loved meeting new people and hearing about how they ended up in prison. The diversity of people was so interesting to me. Crime was not limited to the lower classes, and I met a range of people, with a range of convictions. Some of their stories were so random, but I loved hearing them. I had no idea how true they were, but I didn't care, they passed the time.

My new neighbour was a guy who came home to find his wife in bed with another bloke, so he smashed them both up with a baseball bat. You would think he would leave it there. No, he decided the best way to get revenge was to arse rape the guy. He had no remorse and was quite happy to share this story. I am glad he wasn't my new cellmate.

Wanno had become bit of a celebrity hangout recently. I was introduced to 'Lord Eddie' but he said he preferred 'Fast Eddie'. I had not heard of him prior to his conviction for fraud, when I soon read a lot about him in the press. Fast Eddie was a socialite who hosted notorious parties in London. He made his fortune from these wild sex parties, clubs and property. A friend introduced me to Eddie, telling him I was from Chelsea. We were very different people, but I liked Eddie, his confidence and arrogance were endearing to me. He had some stories, I can tell you. Unfortunately, he became quite unwell, needing a kidney transplant; fortunately for him he was released early because of his health.

During my time at Wanno, other celebrity guests were Max Clifford and Rolf Harris. They both got a lot of stick. Neither were in general population, but I did see them both. I saw Clifford, who had social visits in the church as it was deemed unsafe for him to have visits like the rest of us in the visiting hall. I was off the wing doing some work for St. Giles when I saw him going back to his cell in Seg after a visit. Everyone was shouting at him on the way calling him a nonce. I didn't really understand that. He was a lot of things, but I don't think he was a nonce. Clifford died in Littlehay prison a few years later. I met Rolf Harris when my mate, who was being a handful, was taken to Seg.. He went down to Seg quietly. A screw asked me to help him with his bags. As I entered the Seg unit, there was old Rolf sat on a BOSS scanning chair to see if he had anything up his arse ("Can you tell what it is yet?"). It was a surreal moment. He was a nonce.

Someone else I met at Wanno was someone I admired greatly. Mr David Dein. He was not a prisoner, thankfully; he was a visitor. Mr Dein was the chairman of Arsenal for the great years under Arsene Wenger. Mr B came and saw me. He told me Mr Dein was visiting and asked if I would be part of the welcome party. Of course I would! Mr Dein was visiting Wanno to talk about his new initiative the 'Twinning Project' which would be open to men, women and young offenders in custody, with the aim of preparing participants for release and finding future employment. I met Mr Dein at reception and showed him the way to the chapel where he would be presenting to a group of prisoners, which I was lucky enough to also be invited to. He shared some great stories about his time at Arsenal. I was like an excited schoolboy listening to him. Afterwards he signed a book for me and wished me the best. Who would have thought you can meet your heroes while in prison. I suppose there was a time when you would have had a good chance of meeting some Arsenal players in prison though.

I had been writing weekly letters of complaint to healthcare. I had been in for nine months now, and I still had not been taken to a hospital to have the battery on my pacemaker checked. I could literally keel over if it ran out. For security reasons they don't tell you when you will be escorted to any external appointment. You could arrange a prison break if you knew when you were going. After months of complaining, I was told to stay in my cell and not go to work one day. At about ten I was taken to reception and told I was being taken to an external healthcare appointment. Great. Finally. I was placed in the biggest, thickest handcuffs I had ever seen on my wrists and my ankles, with connecting chains. I looked like Hannibal Lecter. I went through reception with a screw either side of me, we got into the holding area, and we got in a cab! The driver didn't know what the fuck was going on. I started playing up, whispering to myself that I didn't like the driver and that I could get my chains round his neck while he was driving. He was fucking shitting himself, but to be fair to the screws, they encouraged my fun. We arrived at a small hospital in Clapham. The driver said he couldn't pull up outside so he had to stop on the corner, 100 yards from the entrance. Out we jumped and I am shuffling along the road in my chains with a screw either side of me. People stopped on the road in disbelief. It was like a hidden camera sketch. In the hospital, I am booked in at reception. As I sat down, I noticed the waiting room was full of women with newborn babies, half of them breastfeeding. The looks on their faces. They were petrified. One complained to reception and they came over and put a room divider around me! As you can imagine the doctor quickly called me. As I walked into his room, I noticed there was no medical equipment. I have had my pacemaker checked every year for ten years and I knew the routine. But I thought maybe the cardiologist just wanted to chat first to get some more info from me, as I had never been to this hospital before. We sat down and my chains were taken off. The doctor asked what he could do for me. I explained I'd had a pacemaker for the last ten years, I was aware the battery was coming to an end and I needed it checked every six months now, but I hadn't had it checked for well over a year now due to "These bastards." The doctor looked at me confused. He explained he was a podiatrist and I was there to have my feet looked at. I started laughing. I couldn't believe it. I was writing weekly complaint letters about my heart and here I was at an appointment to have my bunions looked at. Luckily, I found the funny side, to the relief of the doctor. I did get some nice new inner soles for my shoes though. When we were done the screw called another cab, and when we left, we had to walk down the road again. I started waving to passers by, fuck with their heads. It was a different cab driver this time. He was funny and called the screws cunts. He told me he had been in Wanno before, too. Top lad. When we got back into the prison I was searched, and my new inner soles were taken off me to be inspected. I never got them back. After this I wrote two letters of complaint a week to healthcare.

In the library I saw a notice to say they held weekly AA meetings in there on a Tuesday evening. I asked a screw about how I put my name down for it, but he told me they didn't run it anymore as the con who facilitated it was transferred. So, I wrote to the CO on the wing and asked if I could facilitate it and start it again. After a couple of weeks I got a reply saying I could, and I was asked to write a list of people and cell locations for them to be unlocked after dinner. For the rest of the week I went around to people and asked if they wanted to come. I told people that although it said AA, it would not be twelve-steps based; it was not their model. It would be a group of blokes talking about addiction. That's it, no serenity prayer. Everyone would 'check in' at the beginning and say how they were feeling, and we would have a discussion after. I got a list of eight blokes, which I thought was pretty good. The first group was good. We each checked in. I got some books from the library about ex-cons who had been through recovery post-release. I read some passages and we discussed it after. It worked. No God. No higher power. Just sharing and building relationships between us. The eight of us became friends and shared books and stories on the wing. More and more people wanted to come and we had to stop at fifteen, as the screws got nervous. They kept a close eye on us through the window. It was always calm. They could see it was a positive group. After a few weeks, someone from RAPt came to observe and brought a load of recovery books and laminated quotes of a load of old shit. I told them it worked as it was our group, with no services with agendas involved and I asked them to leave. RAPt got the arse about it and tried to stop the group. The prison went the other way and asked what else I wanted for the group. I was amazed. I asked for outside speakers. Particularly ex-cons in recovery. A screw took this on, and we had four external visitors to our group. It was powerful. The speakers loved it and so did the lads. I never thought for a second this would actually happen. This group gave me purpose. I would spend the week thinking about what we could do in group. Discuss a topic about recovery. Discuss a book. We even discussed Russell Brand one week, as there was an article in the paper about his recovery. It was a mix of opinion on him. He used too many big words for my liking, just for the sake of it.

I was asked to select my preferred destination for when I was dispersed to another prison. All the C- and D-Cat prisons are outside of London. (Category C are training and resettlement prisons; Category D are open prisons, allowing people to work in the community.) Brixton had a small C-Cat wing, but I was warned off going there. There was a C-Cat prison in Hertfordshire called The Mount and I chose this as my kids lived in Hertfordshire and it was the closest to London. Most of the other prisons were on the coast, too far away from my family. I was asked for my top three prison choices, like I knew any of them. I just gave one. The Mount. After I had submitted the form a screw, who told me she was my personal officer, told me that The Mount did not do buses between Wanno and there. She told me the only way I could get there would be to wait for a transfer and hitch a ride, but this would be a long wait. I said I would wait. Most of my mates had been shipped out already. I wanted to be near my sons so I could see them. I was told they might just transfer me anywhere, but I was willing to take the risk. But this would mean spending more time in Wanno, an absolute shithole, instead of being in more open, clean conditions. I am a glutton for punishment.

Chapter 8

<u>Appeal</u>

"Experience is not what happens to a man. It is what a man does with what happens to him." Andrew Huxley

My solicitor contacted me to say my appeal would be going to a three-judge panel in four weeks' time. My appeal was not based on time received: that had been within the guidelines, although my brief said I should have been sentenced at the lower end of the guidelines–which I wasn't. The appeal was based on the disparity in sentence between my co-defendants and me. Our 'roles' were very different, and they received sentences not much longer than mine. I held no grudges against them. Good luck to them. I really did not hold any hope of a reduction. I had lost all faith in the courts and my representation. I just wanted to get on with things. I was doing well. I had a good routine of running, reading, and work supporting other cons. I wanted to get to The Mount and then to a D-Cat prison as soon as possible. However, I had nothing to lose, so we appealed. I think others had more hope than I did. I told my family not to have any expectations. In the meantime, I would just get on with things. Not that I had a choice.

It is hard to know what to make of people inside. For example, the Polish guy opposite. Probably one of the politest people I have ever met. He would always say "Good morning' to me and ask how I was although he didn't really know me. I was describing him to my friend and said, "What a lovely fella, I can't imagine what he is in for." I also said that he had two teardrop tattoos under his eye. My friend told me that was a sign that he had killed two people. I said I was sure he'd apologised profusely to the victims' families, though.

There was a little old Irish guy along the landing from me. He just talked in riddles. He never actually said anything, just responded with witty quips, the stereotype of a little old Irishman. Anyway, one day we went on a visit at the same time. He was sat with his wife on the next table to me in the visits room. His wife asked him if he would like something from the canteen in the corner of the hall, and he asked for a coffee and a Twix. I was still waiting for my visitor to be processed so we chatted while his wife got his coffee and Twix. When she returned, he sipped his coffee and opened the Twix. Out onto the table from the sealed Twix wrapper falls a small mobile phone and some packs, which must have been drugs. He didn't know what the fuck to do; him and his wife just sat there staring at it. They waved over to a screw and explained they had a surprise when they opened the Twix. I think that was the best smuggle I saw inside. I ordered a Twix on every visit after that.

I received a slip under my door late one night that said I was being transferred to High Point Prison the next day and to pack my things. The next morning, I spoke to my personal officer and explained to her that I refused to go and my reasons why. At first, they threatened to put me on the Seg unit. I held firm and the bus went without me. As a result, I was placed on report and basic regime. The bastards took my TV away, my visits were now only for half an hour, and I didn't get any social time. First thing I did was to rent a TV off a guy I knew who needed the money. I just hid the TV under my bunk until bang-up and then watched it from behind a curtain. I could manage the rest, but I couldn't miss Match of the Day—that should be a basic human right. I was on basic regime for a while, but I never backed down; I wanted to be near my sons, which was more important.

Everything in prison is currency, and everything has a price. You could pretty much get anything you wanted if you had the money to pay the huge mark-up. I wanted a portable CD player with radio to listen to the football. I asked the guy who was known to be able to get stuff to give me a quote. I paid him sixty pounds to get one for me. Yes, this is extreme: but everything has a re-sale value too, so I could sell it on and make most of that back. The risk was, it wouldn't be on my property card, so if they checked that when I moved, they might take it off me. To be honest, it was some of the best money I ever spent. That summer Arsenal reached the FA final. We hadn't won fuck all for nine years. Here I was in bloody prison missing it. I prepared for it though: I bought some hooch from a Polish guy who was brewing it in the laundry. At least the game was on TV, so I could watch it. Just after lunch, we were banged up and I started to drink some of the hooch. It was very sweet, probably to mask the rancid taste. It blew my nut off. For the next two hours I was singing Arsenal songs down the landing. The screws had enough after a while and threatened to take me down the Seg. I didn't stop. What did stop me was going two-nil down. That took the wind out of my sails. But then the boys turned it around and we won three-two. I went nuts. First trophy in nine years. I was thinking about my mates out celebrating without me. After the game I was drunk and emotionally tired. (Arsenal do that to you.) I just feel asleep. I woke up about two in the morning with what felt like a bomb had gone off in my head and the shits. All worth it though. Up the Gunners.

Although there was fuck all to do, it wasn't exactly boring being in prison. There is always something going on and something to moan about. Fights, self-harm, deaths and suicides were daily occurrences. They become the norm. After a while your heart rate doesn't even increase when you see someone stabbed. It's just like when you watch it on TV, like it isn't real. You are just accustomed to it. Humour was dark. I think it was the only way people could deal with the sheer hostile climate we were all in. I saw a guy self-harm badly, cutting his wrists. He casually walked down the landing to the office, blood everywhere. One of the cleaners had a go at him for messing up his nice clean floor. People just did not bat an eyelid at such despair. I heard one of the chefs went nuts, waving around two knives, threatening to stab some screws. We were on lockdown for a few hours so they could manage the situation. At dinner, everyone had the hump as it was supposed to be chip day and we got rice. People's moral compasses were completely off. I don't think we were like this on the outside. I wasn't. We were all institutionalised.

Then you would have the other side of the psyche. The banter, the camaraderie, the funny stories. One night I was laying on my bunk thinking about an old guy who'd died on G-wing. The flap to my cell opens and I can see someone who had covered their face with a pillowcase or sheet and made eye slots. He was shouting through the door at me, but I couldn't make out what he was saying. I was shitting myself thinking it was a ghosting or something (that's when the screws wrap someone up and transfer them to another prison in the night). Then suddenly they ran off. I looked out the little flap and in the gap down the side of the door. I could see someone with a sheet over their head running up and down the landings with a bunch of screws running after him. It was like prison Pac-Man. They managed to catch him; it was my mate Gary, the mad cunt. Somehow the screws left his cell door unlocked during bang-up and he thought he would have some fun. Gary is a fifty-six-year-old married man with three kids. Prison does things to people.

I completed the NVQ with the St. Giles Trust. I was becoming a part of the St. Giles team now, even giving some advice to the team on rough sleeping services. I was asked to do some admin in their office for them, which I was happy to do. I actually read a letter from an old colleague asking the St. Giles team to support one of their clients who was in custody. Funny how things turn out. Each peer worked on the wings that they were located on, but they had a red band position, a position of trust. This person was allowed to move from wing to wing; red bands literally wear a red armband, and the screws will let them in most places within the prison. The current St. Giles red band had been dispersed to another prison, and they asked me if I wanted the position. My first reaction was that I didn't want it. If I could move quite freely throughout the prison, I could be painting a target on my back for people who wanted to move contraband around. Also, cons that have any privileges are seen as grasses. The thinking is they must have been given this position for a reason, such as providing information to screws. After some persuading, I accepted. One reason was that I thought it would help me get my risk lowered and get me to D-Cat quicker. The other reason being I could see mates on other wings. I could go and see Albert, who was still on B-wing. I could also go to the barbershop whenever I wanted. Yes, most prisons have a barbershop. Wanno had two; one was on the same unit as the St. Giles offices and one was on K-wing. I knew most of the lads in there and they would sort me out a trim whenever I popped in. One of the only positives of being in prison is cheap, regular haircuts. You can also have a trim on the wing. Loads of lads were good barbers, and it was a way for them to earn some extra canteen. A trim would cost you a tin of tuna. Or you could apply to go to the barbershop, but you could only go once every six to eight weeks. I went in most weeks for a trim. Some lads tried to get me to move stuff around. I would never actually move anything, but I would pass on messages, some written, some verbal. I wouldn't charge for this. As I said, everything in prison has a price, even this kind of service. I did it to keep on everyone's side and not be labelled a grass.

Back on K-wing, I was to get another new cellmate. Yeah, there is a theme here. I wished I could just get one normal fucking cellmate. Nope. In moves Tom. Another fucking degenerate. He is another racist, but he is also a posh twat. I hate both racists and posh people. He told me he was in for fraud. He told me he'd bought an ex-military aircraft! He said he never paid tax on it and was nicked. I mean, how much disposable income must you have to think, "Might treat myself to a military aircraft"? When I say he was a racist, I don't mean the run of the mill, EDL brain-dead type: he was an actual Nazi. He showed me pictures of his family in SS uniforms, all smiling away at some family event. I dread to think what the aircraft was for. He stupidly told someone on the wing his full name. They googled him and found out he was a Nazi. He went on the numbers straight away. I never see him again.

To say the majority of people in prison are stupid is an understatement, especially in B-Cat prisons. I was in the gym one night, a guy running next to me on a treadmill. He tells me he is in for robbing a bank in Oxford. I ask how he got caught. He tells me it was because of the getaway van. I asked if there was a car chase after the robbery. He said, "Nah, the van was a rental, but they needed ID to rent it, so I gave them my passport details." The old bill must have had a right laugh at that one, the stupid bastard.

People are either stupid, or just weird. I was walking round the yard by myself, in my own little world. Two guys I had never seen before joined me. One was a "High class gigolo" who robbed "two million off an old tart". The other guy strangled his wife "because she is a whore." I said I needed a shit and went inside. I find this ends most conversations.

Back on the wing, I called my solicitor. He told me my appeal had been rejected. The official reply had not been received yet, but the three judges deemed my appeal frivolous. I could appeal again, but if I was unsuccessful I could get more time. I told the solicitor there and then I did not wish to pursue it or hear from him or his firm again. That was it now. I had to accept my sentence. It felt a little liberating. All the court and legal stuff was over. All I had to do now was time. In my head the clock started counting down to release at that point. Before the rejection on my appeal, there was always hope: hope I would win a court battle, hope I would get a lenient sentence, hope my time would be reduced on appeal. Now there was no hope, just time.

There is a saying you hear a lot in prison: "They can lock the locks, but they can't stop the clocks."

Chapter 9

Time

"How you handle your journey will determine your destination."

The problem with everything being done, in terms of sentence, appeal and categorisation was that I was now in the part of my sentence when absolutely nothing happens. Nothing to concentrate on. Just the calendar. The devil makes work for idle hands, so I needed to keep focused and busy. I was reading a lot, three or four books at the same time. I was desperate to do anything to fill my time. The AA groups were still going, but I had taken a step back and allowed others to facilitate it. I would be moving on eventually and I wanted the groups to continue when I was gone. I wanted out of Wanno. Nearly all my mates had been dispersed to other prisons. Mostly to High Point. I would ask about buses to The Mount every week and I kept reminding the OMU (Offender Management Unit) why I wanted to go to The Mount and how important it was for my "eventual reintegration back into society": you must use their language when communicating with them. My twice-weekly letters of complaint to healthcare, however, were being noted and I was placed on medical hold, which that meant I could not be transferred until I had been to the hospital. This was bittersweet. I was worried about my pacemaker, but I wanted out of Wanno.

I didn't have a cellmate for a few days, which was a relief, but I knew one would eventually be coming. I spoke to the screws and told them about my long list of nightmare cellmates, and asked for someone bloody normal for a change. The screw told me they put some people in with me on B-wing because in my file it said I integrated well with people that others find hard to manage. Great! Lucky me. I told the screw some stories of past cellmates and even they found it funny. A couple of days later, I returned to the wing and I could see a group of Polish lads standing outside my cell. I thought they were robbing it. So I ran over and started pushing them out the way. As I looked in the cell, it was dark in there. Darker than normal, like someone had covered the barred window. I walked in the cell, and standing there was the biggest man I had ever seen. He was six foot five and as wide as a barrel. He was blocking the light. The Polish lads outside were laughing and telling me he was my new cellmate. Cellmate? The guy needed a cage. I introduced myself to the big guy, but he didn't speak a word of English. In fact, he didn't speak at all, which was unnerving. Normally, whoever is in the cell first has the bottom bunk. One of the Polish lads said he wanted the bottom bunk, as he was too big for the top bunk. I agreed—fuck having that over me at night. On the landing I could see the screw I'd talked to about having a normal cellmate. He saw me, and was laughing his head off. I went over, and even I saw the funny side. They stitched me right up. All the screws found it funny and they were saying I would be his "bum friend". I started playing around with the screws and the Polish lads, telling them I would fuck the guy up when the cell door was closed. I was shadow boxing on the landing. The big guy came out the cell and the Polish lads were telling him what I was saying. I did it with a smile on my face, so he knew I was joking— this guy could easily kill me. He just stared at me. Later that night we got unlocked for food. I have never seen anyone eat like this man. He got loads of food from the lads working at the servery. People were, rightly, trying to keep him happy. He then ate two tins of corned beef, two tins of tuna and a pack of biscuits. When he finished, he just lay down on his bunk and fell asleep. The TV was on. He'd wanted to watch something on BBC2 while he was eating. Whoever has the remote for the TV in a cell is the dominant one. I was happy to let him have it. But he had fallen asleep with the remote on his chest and the TV was on BBC2. I was on the top bunk; I thought about reaching down and taking the remote, but I didn't fancy him waking up with me over him. As I lay there watching Canals of England, the cell door opened. I jumped down off my bunk and a couple of screws were stood there like a pair of school kids, giggling. They said, "We thought you might need this" and threw in a tub of Vaseline. As the door shuts, the big guy wakes up with me standing there with the Vaseline in my hand. Again, he just stared at me. Thankfully, he just went back to sleep. I didn't sleep very well that night, in fear he would kill me or fuck me. I never found out the guy's name. He was my cellmate for a few nights. His friends told me he was in for selling human organs on the black market. I didn't believe them until he showed me his papers. They were not lying. But one day he was just gone. He went to court and never came back. The whole time he never said one word to me.

A few weeks later, I was on B-wing seeing someone about keeping his flat while in custody. I decided to use the phone on the landing, seeing it was free: you need to take your chance when you can to use the phone. I was talking to my Dad, when what felt like a tree falling on me came out of nowhere. It winded me. I was still on my feet and I spun round ready to fight, and standing there was the big guy. He had a big smile on his face and just said, "Hi, Kurwa." I told my dad I would call him back. The big guy hugged me! He tried talking to me in broken English and asked if I was ready to fight him. He had a smile on his face though, thankfully. From what I could understand, he wanted to come back to K-wing to be my cellmate again. He said, "No fucking." I said he would be welcome to come back if he got onto K-wing. What could I do, I needed my organs?

I already had a new cellmate, however. Not that I told him that. An African guy called Simon was now in with me. I liked him. Finally, some peace. He was a genius at cooking in a prison cell. He had a genius way of heating up food. I say genius, but it was bloody dangerous. I was still impressed. He put his Tupperware box with his food in it into a bucket, and filled the bucket with water. He had an electrical power cable, with the wires stripped free at one end. He put the exposed wires in the bucket of water and the socket into a power source and then he turned the power on! It would heat up his food. He made great curries in his bucket. One weekend he made me a coffee cake. How the fuck does someone make a cake in a prison cell? No key inside though, which I was disappointed with. Bake-off eat your heart out.

I had now been in prison for a year. I couldn't even comprehend it in my mind. A year. I didn't know how I'd made it this far and kept my sanity, to be honest. It had strangely gone very fast, to my mind, but at the same time it now seemed like I had been there forever. It really is interesting how someone can adapt to situations and environments. Friends were saying I was talking differently. They said they had noticed when we talked on visits. I was now talking a mixture of cockney, prison slang, and youth slang. It made me wonder what else had changed in me. I was a lot stronger mentally. I was more confident in myself, too. Not sure why. When on the wing you need to walk with your head up and shoulders back with confidence or you will be predated upon. I was healthy. I had had no drink or drugs for a year (except for the FA cup final day, which I would not be repeating). I was running every day, so I was physically fit and well. I was also more thankful for things I had taken for granted. Family, friends. They were all amazing. They say you find out who your real friends are when you are in trouble. Well, I had some real friends, and my family were just amazing.

Christmas was approaching again. My second in prison. I just hoped it would be better than the last one (which wouldn't be hard). The Christmas adverts on the TV were killing me. Just all food. The St. Giles team had a Christmas work party, which was nice. Lots of food. It was almost like a work party on the outside but with no booze. I filled my boots and was sick after. I wasn't used to that much food and sugar. The St. Giles team wrote me a nice Christmas card thanking me for my help. They'd had a recent audit that I'd helped them with, and it had gone well. The card was a nice touch. It made me feel valued, which I hadn't felt for a long time.

A friend from B-wing was moving over and wanted to cell up with me. AJ was crazy. Obviously, I liked him. We spoke to the screws and they arranged for Simon to move over with a friend of his. I would miss his cooking. AJ was solid and I knew we would be friends when we got out. Funny as fuck. On the first weekend banged up together, he had a visit. I was having an afternoon nap. So, he left a load of breadcrumbs on the windowsill and left the window open. I woke to a fucking pigeon on my pillow, looking at me. I shit myself. I shot out of bed. There were loads of the bastards in the cell with me. I couldn't get them out the window. I was like the birdman of Alcatraz. There was never a dull day with AJ, which was why I was happy to bang up with him. He had a mate next door to us called Ginge. He was mad as fuck too; they were like a comedy duo when they were together. Ginge was having some trouble on the wing with this guy who was threatening to wet him up (stab him). I came back to my cell and all my magazines were gone. AJ had given them to Ginge, who had wrapped them around his arms, legs and torso like body armour under his tracksuit. Ginge wore it for a few days. Thankfully nothing happened. Plan for the worst though. Smart lad.

I read a story in the paper about Brixton prison. During a search they found human shit in a freezer. The shit didn't really surprise me. I knew that some of the kitchen lads put shit in the nonces' and rapists' food over on C-wing. That was common knowledge. What I was intrigued about was, why freeze it? It's not as if it would go off. Did they defrost it before using it? Brixton had to get food sent over from Wanno for a few days. I don't think they would have fared much better to be honest. There were other stories in the press about Wanno, too. One was about smuggled contraband. It was obvious they would spin the cells as a reaction. If you have something you shouldn't and you see something like this in the national press, you hide it well or pay someone to hold it or plug it for you. The search came forty-eight hours after the story. They searched twenty-six cells on my wing. They found twenty mobile phones, loads of drugs and ten toasters! Fucking toasters. Everyone knew the search was coming. Imagine what they'd have found if it had been a surprise search! I also read in the paper that Chris Grayling the Justice minister had agreed to train screws for Saudi Arabia. Poor fuckers. At least they wouldn't need to worry about books if they'd had their hands chopped off.

A great story I heard that wasn't in the press (though I wish it had been as it would have shown the level of pure incompetence at Wandsworth prison): a lad saw a fax machine at the main reception while he was being processed following a court appearance. The fax number was on a handwritten note on the machine, so they had it to hand when people called up and asked for it. This lad memorised it and gave it to a friend on the outside. His friend googled a court document and edited it, stating that the prison must release his mate immediately. The dumb cunts released him without checking the source.

I finally managed to get off medical lockdown because I highlighted the fact that I had more chance of accessing health care at any other prison than at Wanno. My transfer was now being held up because I needed a sentence plan. This a plan about what I would need to achieve during my sentence so as to have a successful integration back into society upon release. I had been in fifteen months, so being told only now that I needed one in order to move was frustrating. Resettlement should start on day one, not at the end or in the middle of a sentence. The OMU department was like a myth. No one had seen them or met an OMU officer. So, I wrote my own sentence plan. I received a questionnaire-type document from OMU. It was dated two months prior to me receiving it. So, it took them two months to get it to me, in prison! Can't blame the postal service for this one. I knew what they would write and how they would write it. I had written hundreds of support plans in my job. I was homeless so I needed to get to a D-Cat prison to work, to save for a deposit for a flat on release. I knew there was no social housing and I would not be priority need, so I would need to rent privately. I wrote an action plan on how I would achieve obtaining accommodation. I needed to be employable, so I wrote an action plan on how to achieve this. Education, then D-Cat, volunteer, references. I wrote it all up and I posted it internally to the OMU department along with the questionnaire they'd sent me. It worked! They typed it up and sent it back to me. My sentence plan was done. I was ready to go. A new start. I was anxious, but I had been at Wanno for much longer than I should have been. I would not miss Wanno. Absolute shithole.

I was in Wanno for eighteen months. This was during a period of change for the Prison and Probation Services. Austerity and cuts had hit the prison system hard. Staff numbers were down forty percent from previous years and they could not recruit any new staff. It was hard enough getting through prison without having to deal with this, too. Every aspect of the prison was hit by cuts. Twenty-three hours behind a cell door for most prisoners was the result, which led to more emotional turmoil, which resulted in more self-harm and violence. I felt I had handled myself well and came out of it with all my faculties. Just. I had hoped the hardest part of my sentence was now over, but I still had a long time left to go, in new environments where I would not know anyone, and no one would have my back like they did at Wanno. I would have a new set of problems.

Chapter 10

The Mount

"Obstacles are often steppingstones."

I was sat in my cell watching the news. The door is opened, and a screw tells me I am moving to The Mount tomorrow morning. He tells me my luck is in as there is a prisoner transfer there for court, and I will be hitching a ride. I have a mix of emotions, as with everything in prison. I am glad I am finally getting out of the hellhole that is Wanno. But in terms of prison, it is all I know. I know which screws are twats and to avoid. I know which cons are twats and to avoid, and I have my social network, who I trust and will miss. I have been lucky, knowing people when I first arrived who vouched for me. I won't have that at The Mount.

I pack my stuff and have an uneasy night's sleep. You hear a lot about C- and D-Cat prisons, like they're the promised land. Privileges galore. I have a few things in my property that are not on my property card. I don't have time to sell them, so I pack it all and hope the screws don't check my stuff when I arrive at The Mount. The next morning, I say my goodbyes. I even get to see Mr B. He was the best screw I met. I get to reception via the induction wing and I take a moment to remember when I first walked onto that wing. Shitting myself and wet behind the ears. I was now a lot wiser on how shit runs inside. I had seen a lot. Spice was something you put in a curry. I had a whole new vocabulary. Ghosted. The Numbers. Spun. Wrapped up. I was walking through that induction wing a different person. A better one, I hoped.

I knew the drive to The Mount as I used to do it regularly to see my boys who lived close by. Being stuck in traffic on the M25 in a meat wagon was new to me though. I had not seen anything green except drugs in eighteen months, but we passed field after field as we came up to Watford; it felt like I was going on holiday. We arrived outside The Mount and we sat there for fucking ages! Ninety minutes sat in the van outside the gate. Finally, we get off the bus, and go to reception to be processed. They call my name and some jovial screw starts asking me questions all nice like... How am I..? Is he special or what? I never got so much as a hello from a screw before. I decide he is trying to get me onside to be his grass or something, so just grunt at him. It really threw me. I am told to put my bags into a trolley and to follow the screw to the induction wing. The Mount is certainly different from Wanno. It feels more like a university campus. I am pulling my trolley along and we come out of the building into an outside area with grass and plant beds. Fucking grass! I follow the screw down some paths, small blocks either side. We come out onto a bigger area of grass. It felt so weird. To you reading this, you are probably thinking, wow, grass. This was like a park in prison. I had not seen anything but crumbling Victorian stone, rubbish and concrete for eighteen months. It was like getting back a sense, like smell. And then, I kid you not, a duck with a row of ducklings behind it walked across the path in front of me. I literally stopped in amazement. The screw sees me staring at the ducks and says, "Oh yeah, we have ducks here." I thought about the Korean guy who cooked pigeons in Wanno. He would have loved it here. The screw tells me the induction wing is brand new and I am one of the first to move onto it. He tells me the cells will have phones in them soon. We get to the wing, which is called Nash Wing. Everything is brand new. It was like if Lego made a prison. The wing was empty. I was told I would be on the "Second floor." "The twos," I replied, and the screw looked at me like I was stupid.

I meet my new cellmate. He'd arrived that morning. His name was Jason, a Jamaican guy who had served fifteen years. He said, "How crazy dis place man, they said we can have a phone, in da cell!" Even I couldn't get my head round it all, let alone someone who had been inside for fifteen years. I settled in and got chatting to Jason, he was sound. He was in his fifties but looked younger than me. He took his top off to change and showed me some bullet wounds. Tells me where he was shot. He got shot on every continent. He tells me he has grown up and has changed his ways. I joked that he must have been a right arsehole to get shot that many times. Jason is the stereotypical Jamaican guy. Everywhere we talk about, New York, Boston, LA, Paris, London, he tells me he has a "baby mother" there. I ask him how many kids he has, and he tells me he can't remember.

The next day the Chaplain comes into my cell and asks me about my religion. I tell him I am an atheist. He looks at me like I have just pissed on his shoes and says, "I don't believe that." I didn't know how to reply to that, so I said, "You have your beliefs father, I have mine." I don't need beef with a Chaplain, but he just would not let it go. He started talking about the beginning of man, the lunatic. When he asked what religion I was I should just have said "Jedi." I left him standing in my cell in a fit of God rage. Every professional I had met at The Mount so far was clearly nuts.

Again, I was to be inducted and assessed on Nash wing. I would not be making the same mistakes as I had when I was on induction at Wanno. In a large group we were told The Mount was now a resettlement prison and we were the first group to come through. The induction was facilitated by a con, a right prick, who thought he was a screw. He walked about with a clipboard, the melt. He started to ask me questions and I told him to do one. So far it was fucking weird at The Mount. The screws were bending my mind; they seemed… normal… You could even have a conversation with one if you wanted one. (I didn't.) During the induction we were told The Mount was a 'working prison' and everyone would need to be in employment or education. I spoke to the St. Giles Trust before leaving Wanno and they told me they had a new contract to provide resettlement support at The Mount. They said they would put in a good word for me to become a peer at The Mount for them too. But when I arrived they told me the resettlement wing was so new the St. Giles team was not yet in place. So, I said I would do some education until they were.

The RAPt team also did an induction session. I said I had been through their program and got a lot out of it. I was asked if I would be a peer for them, but I declined, as it meant I would be placed on the detox/rehab wing. Again, lesson learned from Wanno. I would not be doing that, so I declined.

The Mount was nice; I had so much more time out of my cell and was able to walk the grounds. Loads of grass and benches to sit and just chill. I had had next to no exposure to the sun in months. I was sat on a bench one day by the 'Druggy wing', minding my own business, enjoying the weather. I could see two lads shuffling towards me who were clearly from the Druggy wing. Have you noticed heavy drug users kind of shuffle? They walk faster than most people, but they shuffle? Anyway. One lad had something clenched in his hand; he looked like Gollum in Lord of the Rings, clutching at the thing in his hand. The other lad wanted to see what it was but Gollum was having none of it. I guessed it was a rock of crack or a bag of spice. The lad who wanted to see starts biting at the other guy's hand like a Rottweiler. They start scrapping; the guy is now on Gollum's back, biting his fucking neck. They are thrashing around, and they fall into a pile of gathered-up leaves on the floor. Gollum must have dropped his precious, because he came up with a look of sheer panic on his face. Both lads start to scramble around in the leaves looking for what was dropped. They were on their knees frantically looking though the leaves together. I'm just sat on the bench watching them. After a couple of minutes one of the lads found what they were looking for and he holds it up in the air like he was lifting the world cup. The lads hug and walk off together into the sun like the best of friends again. It was like a little play, just for me.

That night I see one of my mates from Wanno on the six o'clock news. He was a pro boxer and was on trial for allegedly importing forty kilos of cocaine into Britain. He and his three co-defendants were found guilty. I was gutted for him. They were later sentenced to seventy-seven years between them. The news was now like social media for me, getting updates on mates.

My induction was now finished, and I could move off Nash wing. It was a nice wing, everything was new, but I wanted to be in the main prison. I was an enhanced prisoner, meaning I had some extra privileges, so I went to the enhanced unit. As I arrived on the unit, I was amazed to see a snooker table as well as a small CV room which had a couple of cross trainers and running machines. And finally, after eighteen months... I had my own cell!!! No more mad cellmates. I was so relieved.

Soon after I left Nash wing, a story went around the prison about a screw catching a lad giving his cellmate a blowjob on there. I am always asked about this kind of thing. People think there is a lot of man loving going on, whether consensual or not. The only thing like this I ever saw was once, in

Wanno, when a screw let me out of my cell to have a shower before a visit, while everyone was on bang-up. I told him I hadn't had a chance for the past two days and I had a bird visiting me who I fancied. He unlocked me. I walked along the landing and into the shower room. As I walked in, I could see two lads in one cubicle, one washing the other's back. I did a 360 and just walked out. I am not saying it doesn't happen, but I never really saw it or even heard that much about that kind of thing. America is just fucked up. That shit is not commonplace in the UK. Anyway. The Mount spent millions on a brand-new wing. They probably had meetings and votes on what to name their pride and joy. Well, after being open for four weeks, Nash wing had now been dubbed 'Nosh' wing, after the incident with the blowjob. The name stuck and I believe it still does to this day.

I settled into my new wing and was getting to know the lads who were on my landing. I could tell straight away some of them were dickheads. But there were a couple of lads who seemed cool. Everyone asked what I was in for: just what you did not do in Wanno; it was a no-no. There were a lot of differences between Wanno and The Mount. There were the obvious ones: one was a shithole and one was…nice…I suppose. Another was the screws, which I already mentioned. They were pretty much all normal and not roided up to their eyeballs. But there was another big difference, and that was the cons. I could not put my finger on what it was. But they were different. For the first couple of weeks I just could not relate to other cons and form any friendships, even to say hello to someone. It was strange for me. In Wanno I knew a lot of people, I spoke to a lot of people and I got on with a lot of people.

There were a couple of lads on my landing who I could not stand. They were the lads from small towns who sold a bit of weed and a couple of grams of coke down the pub and thought they were Pablo Escobar, who see themselves as big fish. But if they were in Wanno or London, they wouldn't last a day. There seemed to be a lot of lads like this. If you went around Wanno thinking you were someone special, you would be shown you were not. Where you were from was important, too. Everyone in The Mount seemed to be from places like High Wycombe, Bishop's Stortford and St Albans. One lad said he was from "Biggleswade," which I though he made up. Whatever the reason was for not making any friends, I hadn't made any at all. I felt isolated and I actually missed Wanno.

Chapter 11

The Bear

"Nothing ever goes away until it has taught us what we need to know."
Pema Chodron

A few weeks had passed. I was so much more relaxed now I had my own cell and space. However, I still hadn't settled in. I was lonely. I was writing a lot of letters and spending a fortune on phone credit calling friends and family. I had a good routine. I had signed up for a four-week peer-mentoring course. I was running five kilometres every day. I would go to the library most days, as I was reading like I was studying for something. But I was struggling. I spent months waiting to get to the promised land of a C or D-Cat prison. Away from an old Victorian prison to a prison where I would have a lot more time out of a cell. However, I now realised that the environment is not important when you are with people you call your friends. I missed mine. My environment had improved but my personal situation had not. I mean, how the fuck does a grown man make friends in prison? I was worried that the longer I was seen alone, the more chance I would be labelled a loner and then it would be even harder to make any friends. There will be people reading this thinking, "You are in prison, not a holiday camp to make new friends." Prison is hard enough to get through. Without someone to at least talk to, things can go dark quickly.

One day coming back from the library I bumped into an old friend. A friend I knew a long time before I went to prison. I'd had no idea he was in The Mount. He had been convicted of killing another friend of mine. The effect it had had on both families was heart breaking. They were kids. I was too at the time. I saw John sitting on a wall by my wing. I had not seen him for fifteen years. I didn't know what to do, to be honest. I was not sure if I wanted to speak to him or not. I was angry with him, but I'd known his family long before the incident and I had a lot of time for them. John spotted me and came over. He looked a shadow of himself, gaunt and thin. He was dressed in a white robe, he had a long white beard and he wore a little white Kufi hat. He asked what I was doing in there. I explained, but he did not seem to believe me. He seemed very paranoid. John told me he had converted and was now Muslim. This was quite common in prison. I was concerned about his mental health. I had no concern about the fact he had converted to be a Muslim, I hoped that was a comfort to him. He made very little eye contact and he seemed to be distracted. It was a shock seeing him. I said I would see him again soon and left. I had mixed emotions seeing him. As I said, things can go dark quickly in prison. After a few days I saw John and the people he mixed with. I spoke to my personal officer and said I knew him pre-prison and I was worried about him. I contemplated over a few days about John, whether I wanted to speak to him or not. I decided he was an old friend, so I would do it. I found him in his cell, which was also in a bad state. I sat down and I was just honest with him. I told him I was worried about him and worried about the company he kept. John showed me his torso and arms. He had small cuts all over his body. He told me he was cutting out small listening devices that the CIA had implanted into his body. I left him after about an hour. I told him to look after himself and I went and spoke to my personal officer again and reiterated my concern. I kept my distance after that. His 'friends' had noticed my presence around him and clearly didn't want me talking to him.

I completed the peer mentor course. I was told I had to do something, either 'work', or education. I still wanted to work with the St. Giles team (who were still not in place), but I said I would do some education in the meantime. I signed up to an English class as I needed to improve my grammar. My first class, the group was given a short story to read. It was a small book. I finished reading it twenty minutes before everyone else. The teacher told me to read it again when I said I had finished. I say teacher, but he was more a facilitator. When everyone had finished reading the short story the guy asked what everyone thought of it. After a long period of silence, one lad said, "It was deep, fam." One said he would "Fuck the guy up" in the story. And that was it. The class was over. I went back the following day and it was much the same. The 'teacher' had no interest in the lesson or content. He just told us to read something. I could do that in the library. It was clear everyone in the class had different levels of need. I was probably on a much higher level than everyone else in that group and that is saying something. I am dyslexic and my spelling is terrible. This is the problem with education in prison; they do not have the means to meet the level of need. In an ideal world there would be different classes for different levels. But there was not enough funding to do this. I fucked the class off; I was just wasting my time. And I had a lot of it to waste. For a few weeks I just stuck to my routine. But then my personal officer told me I had to work or go back to education. I told him I was waiting for a role with the St. Giles team, but he said I had to do something, as they did not know when the team would be in place, and if I didn't, I would be sent back to Wanno. Most lads at The Mount work for DHL, packing prisoners' canteen for distribution to other prisons. I didn't want to do this as I saw it for what it was. Slave labour. Prisoners work about six hours a day, five days a week for about twenty pounds pay a week! I have no idea how they get away with it. In the end I was forced to take a job with DHL. It was hard graft. Lots of heavy lifting and walking. You are either a picker or a packer. I started as a picker. I would just walk around the stores putting orders together, and then giving them to the packers... to be packed. I have had some shit jobs in my time, but this was as shit as it comes. You couldn't even nick anything as everyone is robustly searched at the end of the shift and they have a tight stock checking system. After a couple of weeks, I was 'promoted' to packing. I fucking hated every minute of it. I wouldn't have minded if I could have saved up some decent money doing it for when I was released. A percentage could be given to you weekly for canteen and a percentage is saved for release. I don't see why the lads could not get minimum wage. Well, I do see why. Modern slavery by big companies. It does happen in this country.

I met with my offender manager. They were a lot more visible than they were at Wanno. (They existed.) I took along all my documents and workbooks in a little file. He seemed a bit shocked at my level of organisation. He said he was really impressed with my level of motivation, as I had completed my sentence plan already. I told him I needed to get to D-Cat ASAP, to work in the community, to save so I had a deposit to rent somewhere when I was released. He agreed and said he would put me forward for D-Cat in a few months. I was pleased I was being listened to and that my hard work was being recognised.

The Mount was a holiday camp compared to Wanno. There were fights now and again but you get that in any environment where you put a lot of people together. Most people wanted to behave to get to D-Cat. However, there was one serious incident. I was on the unit having a game of pool. I could hear a couple of lads arguing at the microwave over rice. Not synthetic cannabis, actual basmati rice. One guy took the glass plate out of the bottom of the microwave, smashed it and used it to cut the other guys throat. There was blood pissing everywhere. The whole prison was locked down and an air ambulance landed in to airlift the guy to hospital. The guy who did it was in on a ten stretch. He would now get another ten on an attempted murder charge. Over a bag of rice. That night on the news, it was reported that someone had died in Wanno over the weekend. His body was not discovered until the Monday morning. I wasn't surprised. I also read that in a prison in Thailand they hold a boxing tournament once a year and the winner is set free. I wondered if they would reduce violence in UK prisons if that was brought in here.

One night I was woken up at two o'clock by what sounded like someone cutting the grass with a lawnmower. I got up for a piss. Suddenly a light is outside my window. I thought, what mad fucker is cutting the grass at two in the morning? I looked out the window, and there was a drone hovering outside it, its light shining in my face. It was like a close encounter of the third kind. Drones have cameras apparently; they would have seen me standing at my window in my pants looking very confused. Over the next few months, I got used to drones waking me up. It was like Heathrow some nights.

The big tree in the centre of the outside communal area had been a talking point recently. A guy was refused a transfer, so he climbed up it in protest. He stayed up there all night, but got what he wanted in the end. Guess what, yep, someone else climbed up it the following day demanding something or other. The screws can't do anything to get them down, so they just wait. I could see the tree from my cell window; hours of entertainment watching the screws trying to get them down. At one point someone was up that tree most days; it was like Planet of the Apes at The Mount for a while. When I walked past the tree, I always looked up into it to see if anyone was up there.

I would sit on the wall by that tree, usually reading in the sun. A lot of the lads looked at me like I was mental, but I liked my little spot. One day this lad comes up to me. He is fucking massive. I have seen him about. He says to me, "I see you training every day, but you are doing it wrong. If you want to lose weight, you need to use light weights not do CV." If this happened in a gym on the out, I would leave that gym and never go back. Someone you don't know, talking to you in the gym, giving you advice, is the worst kind of person (just me?). But as I had no mates and he was fucking massive, I thanked him. He sat down next to me and introduced himself: "Everyone calls me Bear." I said I could see why. Bear told me he was a boxer. I asked if he was a BEAR knuckle boxer..? (No wonder I had no friends.) He laughed and said he had not heard that before, (I lost a lot of faith in humanity that no one had made that pun before) and we just sat on the wall chatting about boxing. Bear was a Spurs fan, but despite this, after that first chat I spent every day with him. He was sound; we got on well. He said he did not like most of the lads in the prison, either. He also said he could not put his finger on why, though. Everyone feared the Bear, but he was quite soft in his personality. He had some problems with his missus, and we chatted about that a lot and his feelings about it all. He was the least aggressive person I knew. That was until I saw him train and do some pad work, when he turned into an animal. Scary as fuck. I felt sorry for anyone who got into the ring with him.

A couple of days later an officer came to my cell and asked me to come with him. He explained that my old friend John was threatening suicide. He said he wouldn't speak to them, but he would speak to me. John had barricaded himself in his cell. The screws would not let me enter the cell even if John or I had wanted that, but I spoke to him through the door for a couple of hours. I spoke to him about his family and growing up together. I reminded him of some funny shit we got up to as kids. John calmed down and agreed to come out if he could call his mum. The screws thanked me, but I told them they were fucking idiots. They should not have let him get that unwell, that desperate. It had been clear to me for a while that he was unwell. I never saw John again after this.

Thankfully, I started working with the St. Giles team. I got out of the DHL workhouse. I was St Giles's only peer, as I was the only person who had the Advice and Guidance qualification. Some lads started the course though, in order to become peers. I was asked to support the tutor in the groups. I was very conscious of looking like someone I would hate, like the dickhead with the clipboard when I was inducted. My old employer had the contract to provide housing support and St. Giles had the contract to do ETE (Education, Training and Employment). I supported the housing team as I knew fuck all about ETE and the education was a joke, so I swerved that. It was funny, as technically I was employed by the company who had recently sacked me, but I was only earning fourteen pounds a week compared to the twenty-five grand a year I was earning before. Funny how things turn out.

Talking about funny. I read a story about a dwarf who was sentenced to nine months in prison. The headline was. 'Dwarf jailed for pretending to be a Dalek'. A four-foot tall, wheelchair-bound dwarf 'threatened' his carer, because he stuck a plastic dart on his head and shouted, "Exterminate!" at her. She called the police! It gets better. The fuckers tasered the poor little bastard, twice!

I would happily have had him as a cellmate. He sounded like a right laugh.

Just as I started the role with St Giles I was told my application for D-Cat would be considered in four weeks' time. I was asked to write a personal statement stating why I would be suitable for open conditions. It felt like I had only just arrived at The Mount, but this was good news.

I had submitted my D-Cat application and was waiting for a reply. I received an appointment to see my offender manager. I sat down with him to discuss my application. Again I was asked where I would like to go, in order of preference. I decided I wanted to go to the new D-Cat wing in Brixton prison. It was close to my family and it would be the best placed prison for me to get work in the community on day release, which was so important to my resettlement. Although Brixton was a shithole, and it would mean going back to a Victorian prison, I decided this was the best path for me. My offender supervisor said it would be difficult to get me to Brixton as, like with the problem I had at Wanno, prison buses did not normally go from The Mount to Brixton. We discussed the other D-Cat prisons. They were all miles from London and in the middle of nowhere, so not suitable for me. I would never see my family and friends. This was noted. My OM said my application for D-Cat was good but there were some negative comments on my file, which might impact on it. I was surprised, to be honest. I asked what they were, specifically, but he said he could not tell me. Compared to most of the other lads, I was an angel. I couldn't work it out. I spoke to a mate who told me you could request your records under Freedom of Information rules, so I did. I received them quickly, which was a surprise. The negative comments were largely from one screw. This guy was a fucking melt. It didn't help that I'd told him this quite often, I suppose. He recorded every encounter with me as a 'Negative'. He said I was arrogant and talked back. I agreed with him: I am arrogant, and I do answer back, and I will tell you, you are a twat. But I am in prison. He is a prison officer. Grow a pair. He recorded on my records that I asked for my newspaper in an 'unpolite manner'—I mean, come the fuck on. I did what I would normally do. I confronted him. I told him I had read all of his negative comments he had written about me. He seemed shocked. I told him that because he was of a sensitive disposition, he was impacting on my rehabilitation and I would be making a complaint against him. He asked if we could sit down and talk about it. I said it was too late for that. I didn't want any problems. I just wanted D-Cat. But if this guy had been in Wanno he would have had shit poured over him every day. I wrote a complaint. Fuck him. A few days later I was summoned to meet with a senior officer to discuss my complaint. It was a strange meeting to say the least. The officer was like a Ricky Gervais character. Sat in his office, I explained why I had made the complaint and why I felt it was justified. The officer said, "I note from your records you were military." I said I was, but for a very short time, and I said I did not see myself as a veteran. He asked me what my military number was. I said I could not remember. He said this was impossible as it was drilled into you. I said I was insubordinate like that. He then proceeded to show me pictures of himself in military dress, telling me he was a sniper. I had no idea what this had to do with my complaint. He then shows me a picture of his wife. She was attractive. He asked me how old I though he was. I said "Forty-two?" he said, "No, I am fifty, my wife is thirty, and I have a six-pack." I am looking round the room for a hidden camera, as this must be a wind-up. He was one of the strangest people I had ever met. He went on to say he did not believe I had been in the military, so he would not consider my complaint, as I was clearly a liar. I was stumped, to be honest. I asked if I could return to my cell to get the proof he needed as I had a document from the Ministry Of Justice (MOJ) stating my military record and number. He agreed. When I returned, he read it and then went on some weird tangent about the military and my lack of respect for it. I said I respected anyone who served their country; I flunked out early, it was just not for me. The meeting ended and my complaint was never discussed.

I read in the paper about a charity for ex-military personnel. It was called Care after Combat. So many ex-military are in prison. 4000 at the last count. Many become homeless, too, which was something I had a lot of interest in. The conversation with the mental prison officer must have stuck, as I wrote to the charity and asked if they would come to The Mount. They responded and said they would, so I wrote to the Governor and asked if he could set it up. He agreed. After the first visit, three ex-military peer roles were created at The Mount. A representative from Care after Combat held a few groups. I didn't attend but I was told they were good. Jim Davidson the 'comedian' helped to set up the charity, but I didn't hold that against them.

Talking of ex-military. There was a guy on my unit. Absolutely gone in the head. He was five foot five, sixteen stone. He was training in the CV room when I was in there. He tells me he has developed his own fighting style from his time in the military and from studying martial arts. He genuinely believes he is hard. When I am running on the treadmill, I can see him punching and kicking the wall. Now I am no expert, but he had no idea what he was doing. He asked if I wanted him to train me: I passed, but I sent him Bear's way to ask him. I thought he would probably get on with the officer who'd been in the military too.

While sitting in my usual spot enjoying the weather, I heard a familiar voice calling my name. It was Albert! I had missed him. We sat and we caught up. He caught me up with all things Wanno. I told him what to expect at The Mount. He said he was surprised how different it was. It was good to see a friendly face. There were not as many Albanian lads at The Mount as there were at Wanno. Albert's reputation had not followed him to The Mount—yet. He had only been here for forty-eight hours. I heard one lad put it on him a bit, and Albert laughed it off when we spoke about it. A few days later the lad had a broken arm and was looking very sheepish. Suddenly everyone knew who Albert was. Over the next few weeks I hung out with Albert and Bear. People who had previously never shown any interest in talking to me suddenly wanted to be mates. I think people were surprised Albert and I were friends. I had no time for this kind of two-faced bollocks. I showed these people the same contempt as they had shown me when I arrived.

I received a letter telling me my application for open conditions had been accepted. I was so relieved. It meant that I would have the opportunity to work in the community, earning a wage to save for a deposit for a flat when I was released. I would also get ROTL (Release on temporary licence). I could have day release and eventually weekend home leave. This was what I had been working towards for two years. I called all my friends and family with the news. The support I had received from them was amazing. Everyone was really pleased for me. I wanted to start to repay their faith in me by getting myself back on my feet.

After speaking to my offender manager, though, there was a catch. I would not be going to HMP Brixton. I would be going to HMP Spring Hill. This was a bit of a kick in the bollocks. It was even further away from my friends and family. The prison was in Grendon Underwood, near Oxford. I wanted to work in London, so that once I was released, whoever I was working for could keep me on as an employee. It was a blow. But I felt I could still achieve what I needed to achieve, and I would soon have ROTL so I would be able to visit my friends and family.

I was given a date when I would be transferred. I said my goodbyes to Albert again. I hoped I would see him again. Bear said he had put in his application for D-Cat, too, so he hoped he would soon be joining me.

I wouldn't miss The Mount. Nice place, shame about the people.

Chapter 12

D-Cat

"We must accept finite disappointment, but never lose infinite hope."

If I'd thought arriving at The Mount was a shock to the system, it had nothing on my arrival at HMP Spring Hill. The journey in the sweatbox was one of narrow, winding Buckinghamshire country lanes. It was the most rural place I had ever been to, little village after little village. Fields upon fields. When the van got to Spring Hill, I did not realise we had arrived. We drove through a small archway and up a driveway to a small barrier. As I looked out the window, I could see a huge manor house with gardens around it. It looked like I had arrived at Downton Abbey. Surely this was not a prison? The van was allowed in past the small barrier and it spun around. I could now see small huts. It had a military feel to it. We were told we had arrived, and we were escorted to reception. The reception area was a small bungalow next to the barrier. As I stood there waiting to be processed, I could see down the drive and for miles ahead. On my right was the big manor house. There were no fences, no wire, no screws, no nothing. If I wanted to just walk off into the fields of Buckinghamshire, I could. It was very surreal. I thought back to when I had first arrived at Wanno, two years previously: intimidating stone walls, fences and barbed wire. And now there was nothing. How had things changed for my situation to improve so dramatically? The only thing that had changed was that two years had passed. This is how they measure risk. Would I have been more likely to abscond if I'd landed here two years ago instead of at Wanno?

We were all processed at reception. As at The Mount, they never checked my property card against what I actually had in my property, which was a touch, as I had loads of stuff that I shouldn't have had. We were taken to the induction hut, which was the first hut opposite to reception and the closest to the big house. I was told I would be sharing a 'room' with someone again. Ah great, here we go again. The huts were like something out of Butlin's. They were small bungalows about fifty feet long. At the front was a TV/social room, a toilet and shower room and a small kitchen. Each hut had two phones at the front. Going towards the back were the rooms, lined either side, about ten each side. I met my roommate, whose name was Mario. Lovely little Italian fella, not Mafia, thankfully. He looked like Muttley out of Wacky Races; he even had the same laugh. We were told our induction would start the next day. The Governor would be meeting us at 10am at the hut. Once people had put their stuff in their rooms, they started to congregate outside the hut. I was sat on a bench just watching people coming and going, or just walking around the prison. The group didn't know what to do. Were we to just stay on the hut? Some of the lads started talking to some of the lads in the hut opposite. They told us we could just walk about as we pleased. Go where we wanted. I didn't trust what we were being told, so I just sat on the bench by my hut. Everyone else fucked off. All I could see was a row of huts the same as the induction hut. It felt like I was back in training in the army. I sat on that bench for about two hours. I hadn't seen one screw during that period. It was so weird. An induction rep did come to see us. The lads had so many questions it was hard to keep up with what he was saying. Most questions were about ROTL. I just wanted to get my head around the regime at that point. He told us there were two counts a day of the prisoners: One in the morning, at breakfast, and one in the evening after dinner. You had to be by your door for the evening count. Other than that, you could roam around pretty much as you pleased. He told us the times of meals, which were served in the canteen on the other side of the camp. (Camp. His word, which I though was weird). Later that night, Mario and I followed the crowd through the camp to the canteen. It was a big place, Spring Hill. Besides the 'Big House' and surrounding gardens, there was a memorial garden with a small water feature, and two accommodation blocks, which I was told were called the 'Browns and the Greens'. You guessed it: one block was brown, the other was green. Better named than Nosh wing, I suppose. I was right in my assessment that the place had a military feel to it. During the second world war, the site was initially used as a base for MI6 and was then a training centre for **Special Operations**. After the war, the Prison Service took it over and converted it. As we reached the canteen, I saw a massive line of about 300 blokes queuing up for their dinner. We joined the back of the queue and waited. I was in HMP Spring Hill for nearly a year. I spent about four months of that time in a queue. It was a constant. You had to queue for everything! You needed the patience of a saint at Spring Hill.

The next morning, we gathered in the TV room to meet the Governor. I thought it was a nice touch that he met with all new prisoners. It wasn't. He just wanted to threaten us. He came into the room, big fat guy in a suit, full of himself. I instantly didn't like him. All he spoke about was absconding and the consequences of it. I honestly did not see the point in anyone absconding. Even if you had a bit of a stretch still to do, where are you going to hide for the rest of your life? You would be caught, and you would get more time and never be allowed back into an open prison again. Everyone just wanted to ask about ROTL. It was clear to me that this was not on the Governor's agenda. He batted away most questions about it, which was a worry. It was the only reason everyone was here. He told us we must do at least two weeks normal prison jobs like laundry and kitchen work. Also, we would be 'stood down' for a period of three months to asses our risk and needs, during which time we would not be allowed to leave the prison. I thought I had just spent two years looking at my risk and needs. After, we all had more questions than we had had to start with. I convinced Mario to sign up for gardening for the next couple of weeks with me. The weather was great. I knew fuck all about gardening, but it was better than the other options of waste disposal, or the kitchen. The gardeners dressed in green overalls and green caps, and it amused me greatly to see Mario dressed like this, and he did see the funny side, too. He got a lot of stick from the lads about it, calling him Luigi. The two weeks passed quickly. Mario and I just hid and sunbathed all day. I had an interview to be the orderly for the resettlement team, run by a company called MTC NOVO, a Community Rehabilitation Company (CRC). They were the team who supported prisoners with post-release resettlement. I was offered the role and started the next week.

At the same time, I was moved off the induction hut to the main huts. I was worried about who I would pad up with. A friend who I knew from Wanno worked in reception and did allocations, so I had a word in his ear asking for someone normal. He said he had just the person. He took me over to K-hut to meet Clarke. He was the same age as me, and his offence was very similar to mine. We were both happy to pad up together. I loved Clarke, nice guy. Always laughing. Clarke, Mario and I started hanging out together. K-hut was a fucking nightmare, though, as there were a lot of young lads on there, and Rap music played twenty-four hours a day. It was like I had landed in Brixton. It became clear it was a free-for-all at Spring Hill. So much went on around the camp. Drink, drugs, even girls.

Everyone who is new to a prison has it put on them, to see how they react. I was waiting for mine; I knew it was coming. The young lads on my hut could tell I was not intimidated by them. If you were, you would be walked all over for the rest of your stay. I remember in Wanno. There was this guy on H-wing. He was fucking massive; he looked like John Coffey in The Green Mile. One day this skinny crackhead went into his cell and smashed him up with a wooden table leg and stole his canteen off him. The big guy did nothing about it at all. The next time I walked past his cell he had nothing. People took everything off him because they knew he would not do anything about it. And this guy was massive!

There were two brothers on my hut who had been giving me the look. Clarke warned me and said they had it in for me because I told them to turn their shit music down one night. So I was waiting to see if they would put it on me. If I backed down, I would be fucked. I was in the games hut playing pool when they came in with a couple of other lads. I was playing pool; they tried to jump in front of people waiting to play so I told them to do one. They were only there to put it on me, so I decided to just get on with it and not do the whole peacocking. The two brothers were trying to intimidate me with "Bluds, Fams and Murks." I had heard it and seen it all before. One picked up a pool cue and came at me. I stood my ground. I didn't move an inch. These kinds of lads are all mouth. It is true what they say, worry about the quiet ones. These kind of lads are big hard men in groups, but once on their own, they have fuck all. They always reach for a weapon, too: they can't fight. I said I would fight one of them. Any one of them. One on one, outside. No weapons, no mates, just toe to toe. I stood outside waiting. They knew they could not jump me now as I had called them out in front of everyone, so if they did, they would lose a lot of face. They came out as a group and did the usual gesturing. They decided to "Allow me". I stood my ground. People now knew I would stand up for myself. I didn't want to fight, but if I had to, I would.

A charity event was organised for Macmillan cancer research—Brave the Shave. Clarke and I took part, as did most of the camp. £650 was raised, which was amazing, considering we all earned nine pounds a week. The camp did resemble the film Alien 3 though. I have kept my head shaved since this event. My barnet did not survive prison, unfortunately.

After a few weeks, it was apparent to me that I hadn't landed in the dreamland of a D-Cat prison. No one was getting ROTL. It was a period of change for ROTL policy because Spring Hill had had some recent incidents: one prisoner had killed an ex-prisoner while on release. Someone else burgled a local house while on release. As a result, no one was getting any kind of temporary release, whether for resettlement, day release, weekend release or even work. I was really concerned as I was in D-Cat to get paid work. As were most people. Some people did not really need it; they had homes to go back to on release, and businesses or employment. But many, like me, needed resettlement while in D-Cat or we would be released with nothing. I never fully understood why recall/reoffending numbers are so high, until I was at Spring Hill. The odds are stacked against you not bouncing straight back in. This is largely due to the poor resettlement support while still in custody. I spoke to my offender manager, who assured me that by the time I was eligible for ROTL in two months' time, the issues would have been resolved, and I would be able to access work in the community, as long as I did not do anything to increase my risk.

Another concern was the CRC team. I was working as an orderly with them, to support people to access accommodation after release. The CRC team knew nothing about housing. Nothing. They were from an education background. They had no contacts with accommodation providers or any local authority. They knew nothing about priority need or the homelessness act. I was the only one advising people on their post-release options. Most people, being young, single men, would not be of priority need for local authorities. The only viable option would be PRS (private rental sector) properties. However, many, like myself, did not have a deposit. Therefore the need to get work while in open conditions, to save for this deposit. There are charities that can support prisoners to obtain deposits, but CRC had no links for this. The problem is, unless you are from the area local to an open prison, you cannot retain any employment post-release. Very few at Spring Hill were from the surrounding area. In terms of PRS, people are then looking at landlords who will accept DSS (Housing Benefits) and then you throw in LHA (Local Housing Allowances), which is a cap on what a local authority would pay towards your accommodation, and you have a very complex picture—that is without throwing in convictions checks, which landlords were increasingly doing. I was trying to support people to get accommodation, with no phone or Internet access. I would write up an accommodation support plan, and then hand it over to the CRC team. But how could they support people to access PRS properties if no one was getting any day release? It is impossible. As a result, so many people were being released homeless. It was a huge concern to me that I was in a prison designated for the resettlement of prisoners back into the community, that could not get people out on ROTL or find them accommodation upon release, both of which I needed.

As part of my resettlement I did some courses with the National Careers Advisers at Spring Hill. The first course was disclosure of criminal convictions. I was told I would always have to disclose my conviction for the rest of my life to any employer, as my conviction carried a sentence of over four years. The nature of the work I wanted to get back into, I knew I would have to do that, as I would be working with vulnerable adults. But personally I don't agree that someone should have to disclose any convictions unless it is relevant to the job they will be doing. Why should you have to disclose a drugs conviction (if sentenced to more than four years) if you're applying for a job as a scaffolder? It is another barrier to employment and of no relevance. It is discrimination.

As I said, I knew that I would have to disclose my conviction to an employer, due to the nature of the work I wanted to return to. However, the second course was about employment. I told the tutor I wanted to return to the homeless sector once released. She said this was not achievable and advised me to train for a new career. I disagreed with her.

Obviously, I would not walk back into a job, and not at the level I was at before my conviction; but I knew many people working in the homeless sector had criminal convictions. Most people had them prior to becoming a professional but I didn't see the difference. It became an issue between the NCA tutor and me. In sessions she would talk to people about careers in the construction industry, rail and retail. I found it insulting on everyone's part. There was a lot of talent in the room. Yes, most people put their talents into criminality, but the transferable skills were there. If someone said, "I want to be an astronaut," then I felt the NSA should be supporting them to achieve this, not saying, "Have you thought about bricklaying?"

They would not accept I could achieve my goal and I would not accept I couldn't. They contacted my offender manger and said I was sabotaging any support they could offer me, as my employment aim was unachievable. I was expected to engage with NCA for the rest of my stay at Spring Hill. My offender manger agreed with NCA. I told him I would ideally like to work in the community with this aim of returning to the sector in mind. He did not support this. Both the NCA and my OM told me my career in the homeless sector was over, and I needed to work toward an alternative career.

I was beginning to feel really disheartened. I wasn't owed anything by the prison system. But I felt I had done everything asked of me. I had adhered to all the rules and behaved myself. I just wanted them to empower me to get my life back on track. I was beginning to worry about my future and what it would look like. I was a thirty-four-year-old con with no employment prospects, no savings and no home.

Chapter 13

ROTL

"The bird of time has but a little way to fly. And lo, the bird is on the wing." Rubaiyat of Omar Khayyam

I was now in a routine again. Routine is important in prison; it keeps you focused and helps to pass the time. My fitness regime intensified. Spring Hill had a huge field at the top of the camp, which looked out over Bedfordshire. You could see for miles. As the name Spring Hill suggests, the camp is on a hill. I would go to the field every night after dinner and run. I ran between five and eight kilometres every night, depending on if I had been to the gym during the day. After my run, I would shower, then go back to the field to meet with Mario and Clarke for a walk. We would walk around and around that field every night until it got dark.

All sorts went on, on that field. I regularly saw girls meeting guys on there for a bunk up. There was access from a nearby road. One night I saw a lad I knew called Liam walk across the field and just keep going; he was like Peter Rabbit jumping over hedges. He just kept walking. A lot of lads would disappear off camp, but they would come back before evening or morning count. But Liam never came back. They did not realise he was missing until well after the count. By that time, he could have been anywhere. The next day he was on the local news; they said he had absconded from the prison. This didn't help the ROTL situation for anyone.

Stories of people 'escaping' seemed to be daily. People were really pissed off about the ROTL situation. Forty percent of prisoners who came to Spring Hill were returned to closed conditions for breaking the rules. The numbers were so high. People like me behaved themselves to get to D-Cat, then realised there was no resettlement/ROTL, so they thought, fuck it. Might as well enjoy myself, what have I got to lose?

There was a news report about another lad absconding from Spring Hill. What the press did not know was that a prison officer drove the guy to the train station. I shit you not. I knew the guy. He volunteered in the community, he had been at Spring Hill for quite a long time, and he had had enough. He had been waiting months to get day/weekend release to see his kids. He went to reception and said he needed to be dropped into Oxford for work. It was his day off, but they never checked. The prison driver drove him to Oxford station. Funny enough, there was no mention of this in the press, but everyone on camp knew what had happened. The ROTL situation was a catch-22: people were absconding because there was no ROTL, and ROTLs were being stopped because people were absconding.

One night, while walking around the field, Clarke told me a mate of his from HMP Bullingdon was coming to Spring Hill. He said I would really get on with him. He said he was from the same area as me. Clarke was from Bournemouth, so he thought everyone in London knew each other, so "my area" was probably just London, I thought. He said his mate was posh, went to Oxford, and he thought his dad was a lord or something. My first thought was, I am going to hate this guy. A few days later, Clarke introduced me to Oscar. My back was up a little as I had already formed an opinion of him. He quickly changed that opinion. We hit it off straight away. He knew a lot of the lads I knew in Wanno, despite not serving time there. He went to pubs and bars I did in Chelsea, he had exceptional taste in music and despite being posh, knew more cockney than I did. He was so confident and brash in his statements and opinions. I fucking loved it. He was serving a ten-year sentence for importing Class A drugs. You would never have thought it meeting him. We were inseparable from that point.

I have mentioned before that prison is full of people who should not be in prison. D-Cat was no exception. In fact, it seemed like there were more people in D-Cat for white-collar crimes than anything. A guy I met, his crime wasn't exactly white collar, but it was one of the craziest I had heard. Ali told me he was in for "Election fraud." I had no idea what that was. Ali said he owned two properties with his family, which were geographically in close proximity, but in different boroughs. During the general election they voted in the wrong borough. The authorities noticed and arrested Ali and his family. Ali was sentenced to serve six months in prison and his father also got six months and was in the process of being deported from the country. His mother and sister were also sentenced to six months in prison, and they shared a cell. I am sure there was more to the story, but how can a whole family be sent to prison when there is no victim? No wonder prison numbers are so high.

I heard so many insane stories about why people were in prison. I took most with a pinch of salt. But some were just too weird to not be true, if that makes sense. A guy called Pete on my hut. We got chatting about our convictions. He said he was in for possession with intent to supply, too. He showed me his papers; I didn't ask to see them, I think he just wanted to substantiate his story. Pete tells me this story about how he got nicked. Pete had been in prison before for importing drugs; he was well known to the police. One night he meets a bird in the pub, they get on and they start to see each other. They were seeing each other for months. One night the bird asked him to get her some gear as she wanted to party. Pete gets it for her. At the end of the night, while in bed, the bird puts a pair of handcuffs on him. Not in a role-play way. She is a fucking copper! She nicks him! She gets sacked for sleeping with him and taking drugs. He gets convicted for dealing and sentenced to four years in prison. I know dating is a minefield, but Jesus! I have no idea how true this story is, but it is a good one.

Mario was also in for possession with intent to supply. He was at a wedding; a friend asked him to get some gear, he made a call, got three G's for him. Later that night, he had a barney with his missus, the police were called. He got nicked, they checked his phone while he was in custody, and they see the messages from the dealer and then to his mate. They nicked him. He got three years. That is how easy it is to get sent to prison. People will have their own thoughts on whether Mario and people like him deserve to go to prison. Personally, I don't. Yes, he broke the law, but circumstances need to be taken into consideration. Was Mario a 'drug dealer'? Did he deserve to go to prison?

I had now been in Spring Hill for three months. My 'Laydown' period had finished, so I was able to apply for work in the community and day release. I completed some forms about the type of work I wanted to do and the relevance it would have to my resettlement. A couple of weeks passed; I had not received a response, so I went to speak to the team that arranged for work placements. They told me they had looked at my file and noted that I had no GCSEs. OK... I didn't know what they were getting at. They explained that the policy of the prison was that if you did not have at least Level 2 in English and Maths, you would need to get these prior to applying for work in the community. I was fucking gobsmacked! I had been in prison for two years, three months of them at Spring Hill, and they tell me this now! By the time I had obtained these qualifications I would be ready for release. Level 2 in English and Maths would be no good to me if I was sleeping on the streets. I just walked out in a rage.

I had no idea what to do. I needed to be pragmatic. I needed to get around the policy so I could get work. If I left prison with no savings, I would be in big trouble. I had a plan. Next door to the CRC hut was the education hut. I knew some of the lads who were orderlies for the education department. I played badminton with one of them. I went to see him and explained my problem. I asked him, for a price, if there was any way the system could be changed to say I had completed Level 2 for English and Maths. He said he did not have access to the computer system. However, he made the certificates for people who had passed the courses and he laminated them. Education was provided by Milton Keynes College and it so happens that they also provide the education for The Mount. For the price of two packs of burn, eight pounds, he made me two certificates for Level 2 in English and Maths. He asked me if I wanted a qualification in plumbing too, but I declined that offer. The next day I went to the work department. I showed them my two certificates and said I had completed the courses at The Mount. The lady said this happens sometimes, that the records were not updated; she updated my records on the system to say I had the qualifications required to apply for work in the community. Some people have thousands of pounds of student debts to pay for qualifications. Mine cost me two packs of tobacco.

The saying goes: It is not what you know, it is who you know. I had to do something. Yes, I was pretty pleased with myself for using my initiative to get what I needed. It was probably wrong to do it, but needs must. If I had been told at any point while in custody that I would need these qualifications to get work in the community, I would have done them.

In prison there is always a way to get around things. If you needed something there was always a way to get it. At Spring Hill it was a free-for-all. You name it, people had it. I would regularly walk into the TV room on the hut and the lads would be eating KFC and drinking alcohol. I saw a couple of screws chase a couple of lads across the field; they never caught them, but the lads dropped a bag with thirteen kebabs in. Absolutely everyone had a phone. Although most people had them in enclosed conditions, too. Most people had computer consoles. I didn't have a phone. I knew if I were caught with one, it would be straight back to closed conditions. I did have a USB stick though, on which I had films and TV box sets. Obviously, this was not allowed, but it was just to pass the time, nothing sinister. The stuff I craved, which I could not get, were basic things not of a contraband nature. I wanted some decaf tea bags and Marmite. I would have liked a tea before bed, but then I would struggle to sleep due to the caffeine; and I loved Marmite, which was banned in prison, as it was full of yeast, which can be made into hooch. Anyway, the ladies at CRC were sympathetic to my cause. They brought me in decaf tea bags and Marmite for the office. I had my own mules. Bringing in not drugs or alcohol, but tea bags and Marmite.

Although I was so far away from London, my friends and family still made the effort to visit me. The prison was so difficult to get to, I was told, unless you drove. Getting clothes approved and then into the prison via the official means was a nightmare. It had to be signed off by like three officers. I just asked visitors to wear something of mine from home, like a jumper or a jacket, and then they would leave it on the chair when they left the visit and I would just put it on after they left. One visit, I went in a T-shirt and came back with a jumper, jacket, hat and sunglasses. Around this time, Kelly visited me. She was back from Australia and was living back home in Ireland. It had been about a year since I had seen her. We spoke on the phone a lot and wrote but this was the first time I had seen her since she visited me in Wanno. I had changed a lot. I had lost a lot of weight and I had no hair. The visit went too fast, it was hard seeing her, and I missed her. I had blocked everything with regards to girls or relationships out of my head for the past two years. A lot of feeling came back. I was now starting to think about what I wanted when I did get out. I had eight months left to serve and I should get weekend leave soon.

One lad's mother was seriously ill, so he put in a 'special purpose leave' application to visit his dying mother. The Governor refused it. He was heartbroken. He decided to abscond to see her. Unfortunately, she died before he could see her. He handed himself into the local police station. It was in the press. It was reported at court the judge "Condemned HMP Spring Hill," for not allowing him to see his dying mother. The court gave him no further time to serve as a result.

Keeping yourself occupied was difficult. There was only so much exercise and reading you could do. The lads started to go to Bingo on a Friday night. I wasn't having any of that at first, but I relented in the end and went. I won seven pounds the first two weeks. That was nearly a week's wages in prison. The winnings would be added to your canteen spend. With this and my Marmite, I was living the dream. The cons ran the Bingo. Everyone who attended had their names added to a hat; names were drawn for who would call out the numbers for each game. One night a lad's name was drawn who had a strong accent and a speech impediment. He struggled to say the word "four" and could not say "five" at all really. I felt sorry for the guy, fair play to him for stepping up, but it was one of the funniest things I have ever seen. I was on the floor laughing as every number that he drew had a four or a five in it. "Fifteen–fifty-one– forty-five–five." It was like a Morecombe and Wise sketch. We had to abandon the game as everyone was just rolling around. These were the kind of things that kept me sane.

The situation at Spring Hill had become toxic. No one on camp was getting out. The prison published some stats about how many people were getting out and everyone knew they were bollocks. There was a small handful of people getting out and everyone knew who they were. What they did to bump up the numbers was recording every time a prison driver went out to pick someone up or drop them off as a ROTL. People had been at Spring Hill for seven or eight months and not had a day release or any work of any kind. The Governors and the OMU promised things would improve, but people were getting impatient. The camp was at boiling point. I wrote to the Inside Times, a national prison newspaper, about what was happening at Spring Hill. The letter did not have my name on it, as I am not stupid. The letter was printed. A lot of lads cut it out and put it on notice boards around the prison. It caused quite a stir; the screws were trying to find out who wrote it. I never told anyone it was me. A couple of weeks later, the MOJ visited the prison to investigate the many letters of complaints to them about the prison. The word on camp was the Governor was in the shit and clinging to his job. I hoped I had something to do with that.

The good news was, Bear had arrived at Spring Hill. I was writing to him, keeping him updated about the ROTL situation. At least his expectations were low when he arrived. It was good to catch up with him. It was good to catch up on news from The Mount. He told me about a guy we knew at The Mount called Mark. I told Bear I didn't trust him. He said he was in for theft, but I was convinced it was a sexual crime as all he spoke about was women and sex. He was a weird cunt. Anyway, Bear told me he went to Mark's cell to borrow some sugar and noticed something under his bed. Mark had made a sex manikin. He stuffed a laundry bag with sheets. At the bottom he cut a slit where he placed two rubber gloves filled with water, tying the fingers together to replicate a vagina, and at the top of the bag he had spaced two bowls to replicate tits. Bear asked him what the fuck it was, Mark said he made it and fucked it every night with lube. Bear punched him in the throat and never spoke to him again. As I said, weird cunt, Mark.

Things were starting to change. Clearly the visit from the MOJ had had the desired effect. The Governor called a camp meeting, and everyone met in the canteen. The Governor said he understood the frustration with regards to the lack of ROTL. He said they had now been given more autonomy to approve ROTL. He said there was a lot for the OMU to do now, but he encouraged everyone to put in new applications for ROTL and they would approve as many as possible. You could feel the weight lift off people. The atmosphere in camp changed for the better overnight.

I submitted new paperwork for ROTL. Work was my main need, but day release was something I and many others really wanted. Time to spend time with family outside of a prison. The difficulty was, my family were in London, and I would not have the time to get down to London and back on a day release. My sons were closer, in Hertfordshire. The prison wanted to know the ins and outs of a duck's arse when it came to day release. Exact times, route, and destination. As well as exactly what you will be doing when you reach that destination. For a lad from London with no Internet access, it was not easy. I had to rely on family and friends to get the information I needed. Imagine not having that support. What do you put on a ROTL resettlement form if you have no family or friends?

I applied to be collected by car by my sons' mother. (I hate the term baby mother.) We would drive to Oxford where we would have some lunch and go to the cinema. This may sound a strange thing to do on your first release: sit in a dark room where you cannot talk. But the new Star Wars film was out. I was desperate to see it and I had always gone to see these and the Marvel films with my sons. When you leave the prison for any reason, you must have the mobile phone that is provided to you. It is a cheap burner phone but they can track you on it and obviously reach you if needed. You are also given a locker at reception. In this locker was a mobile phone charger, which was plugged in behind the locker. When you return you would put the mobile back in the locker at reception.

There is very little you can do on day release. You can't go to a pub or any establishment that resembles a pub. Money is an issue, too. I had fuck all. I managed to get hold of some from a friend, who sent it to my sons' mum so I could buy us lunch and pay for the cinema. The prison doesn't give you pocket money. You can apply for some from your personal spends account, but with an income of nine pounds a week, which you need to buy phone credit, stamps and products, you would need to save for a year to buy a large popcorn and drink in a cinema.

When the day came, I was excited to see my sons. Before I went to prison, I was close with them. They stayed with me every weekend. But I had been away for over two years. They were both teenagers now. I was worried how this would affect our relationship. They visited when they could with their mum, who, to her credit, was an absolute star throughout. But my absence must have had an effect, probably one I could never measure. I never told my sons why I was in prison. All I said was "I did not hurt anyone, I got involved in something I shouldn't have." That was it. I felt that was all they needed to know at the time. I wondered whether, now we were not in a prison environment, they would want to know more. How would I explain it to them? I didn't think I could explain it if I wanted to. But I did not need to worry. My boys were great with me and showed a lot of maturity. We had a great day. It was strange for me being in public. Something that took me time to adjust to was being vigilant. In prison, you need to know what is going on around you at all times. Every time you step out on a landing, you are doing a risk assessment in your head. You are watching everyone, their body language. You need eyes in the back of your head, and you need to listen to your gut instinct. You can step out on a landing and feel the tension and testosterone sometimes and know it is going to go off. I remember standing in a busy area outside the cinema waiting to go in on that first day release. My eyes were darting everywhere, assessing the risk around me. I didn't need to do this in public to the level I did in prison, but I was so used to doing it, it was hard to stop. I was conscious of it that day and even for many months after I was released. The hardest part of day release is going back to prison. I had found it hard after visits when I was in closed conditions, but I would be depressed for days after a day release.

Chapter 14

Home leave

"Regret is proof of soul."

I had to move off K-hut. Tensions were high between some of the lads and me. My patience was being tested all the time. Snide comments and looks. In some ways I just wanted to fight one of them to get it out the way. I was being provoked. There were five lads who knocked about together. I knew if I had a scrap with one, they would all jump in. I didn't want to move; I was stubborn. I also didn't want to lose face by moving. But in the end I decided I just didn't need it any longer; I was close to my home leaves and getting work. Getting into a fight would compromise that. These lads would bounce back in to closed conditions soon because they were just thick as shit. I wanted to stay with Clarke but he agreed it was probably best to move off the hut. I spoke to a screw and requested a move. I made an excuse about the damp in the hut, and it being bad for my health as the reason I needed to move. I moved over to L-hut and in with an old traveller called Mick. He was quiet as a ghost and he slept like a teenager. I can sit in silence with the best of them but getting a conversation out of Mick was impossible. From what I could tell, he had no interests at all. He did not like football, he was illiterate, did not like boxing or horseracing. I started stereotyping, asking if he had been to Appleby Fair. "Nope, never been." I mean, come on, what traveller does not like boxing and horses!? I was losing hope in finding any common ground with Mick. But one day I put my Johnny Cash CD on and lo and behold, he loves JC as much as I do. I liked Mick. We didn't have many deep conversations. The man loved to watch TV. He would watch anything. Period drama, quiz shows, talking donkeys, he didn't care.

Mick was released and I had another new roommate. Ah man, the minute I met him I knew he would be a nightmare to be around. The guy was a lifer, old-school villain. He had served seventeen years, the whole time being in a single cell. Now he was in with me. His mind had gone. I felt sorry for him, but I didn't like him. I was trying to be understanding; he must have felt like a fish out of water. He constantly talked to himself, even in his sleep, when he would shout out, "I am going to fucking kill you, you cunt!" It was very disconcerting. That is, when he did sleep. He averaged about four hours a night. It was clear he was not used to sharing a space, as he would make so much noise when he got up at 5am. He would put the TV on at 5am. His hearing was poor too, so it was always loud. It felt like I was in Guantanamo Bay getting tortured.

Security was low due to staff shortages. People were not just leaving the camp at night now, they were going during the day. I was invited to Pizza Express for lunch one afternoon. I didn't go, but ten lads I knew did. One came back with a fucking Pizza Express balloon that they give the kids. People were just taking the piss. When I went for my run around the field, fast-food wrappers were blowing around everywhere. Drink and drugs were everywhere, too. There were hut parties most nights. One night, a screw caught two lads coming back into the camp across the field. They were wearing balaclavas; they just beat the screw up. Staffing was just too low; they knew it, and so did we.

One lad who everyone called 'Gums' and who really fancied himself took some spice at one of the hut parties. The lads found him in the showers fully clothed, ranting away to himself, so they put him to bed; but a couple of hours later, during the night count, he was not in his bed. The screws were looking all over camp for him. They found him on the field naked, furiously wanking and pounding away at his arse with his fingers. The lads who were on the Greens were watching him doing it out of their windows. We never saw Gums again; I am not sure if he got wrapped up or requested a transfer. Either way he couldn't show his face on camp again.

I was requesting a work placement most days at the OMU and the Activities Hut. Some people were getting work, but it was work placements they had sourced themselves via family and friends who owned local businesses. The prison had no work placements that they had sourced themselves. None. It beggars belief. I did wonder what the hell the Activities Hut actually did, as there were no activities. What was annoying was that the white-collar crew were getting placements. They started getting paid work and attending Oxford Brookes University. The white-collar criminals always got treated differently. They were given more privileges, and access to the best positions. There was an argument they needed this the least. I subscribe to this. Many did not commit crime because of need but greed. They had homes and businesses. They had a good education. They did not need any more education. They did not need employment as much as people who had few prospects when they were released. The white-collar crew should have been at the back of the queue, but they were always prioritised.

While I was waiting for a placement, I signed up for a business start-up course, run by a charity called Bright Idea. I had had an idea for a business for a while, so I thought, fuck it, why not do the course; I could do it even if a work placement transpired. At the end of the course you present your business idea to a panel that can provide business start-up funds of up to twenty grand. I believed everyone had a business and a book in them. I wrote a business plan for a social enterprise café for the homeless, called the Second Chance Café. The café would use donated end-of-life products to create meals, not only for the homeless but for paying customers too. Bringing together people who wanted to make a difference, whether this was just buying a coffee, the profit from which would go back into the community, and people who needed support. For me, if I was unemployable. I thought I would just be self-employed and still do the work I wanted to do.

Due to so many people being sent back to enclosed conditions, I was flying up the waiting list to move to the Greens. The Greens was a building as opposed to a hut. It was single rooms with more privacy and space than in the huts and it was next to the field. As Clarke, Mario, Oscar and I all landed pretty much the same time, we would be moving over around the same time. Every day there was a story about someone being sent back to enclosed. Every time the question was, "were they on the Greens or the Browns?" because if they were, you would be one step closer to moving onto them. My time would come soon. But before I moved, I had a right old tiff with the old boy. He shouted at me one night as he said I was snoring. I told him to fuck off and not wake me up again. We argued. He rolls over, goes back to sleep and starts snoring. Everyone snores, talks, walks, or farts in their sleep. Everyone! Anyway, the next morning the silly old cunt puts it on me. Right up in my face. He was a game old boy; he was like seventy years old. He said I had disrespected him. I just said respect went both ways. He was obviously someone thirty years ago but not any more. It carried on for a couple of days. It was frosty in the room. I was in a lose-lose situation. If I chinned him, I'd have chinned a pensioner and I'd look like a right cunt. If he chinned me, I'd have been beaten up by a pensioner. What do you do!?

The cellmates I had!! Jesus, I had had some characters in with me! I moved over to the Greens a couple of days later. No more room mates. I had my own room on the ground floor, by the back exit right next to the gym and the field and, even better, Oscar was two doors down. It would have made an excellent episode of Location, Location, Location.

My second ROTL was to a hospital. I had requested more day releases to see family, but they had been declined for no reason that I could tell. When asked why they were declined, the response you would get was "Due to local policy" which seemed to overrule the National PSI (Prison Service Instructions). Basically, the rule was "Whatever the Governor says". The hospital appointment was to have the battery in my pacemaker checked, which had still not happened, two years and three months later. I mean, it would be nice to do my time, get out and not die because the battery in my pacemaker ran out. Healthcare made an appointment for me at a hospital in Oxford. The Cardiologist was amazed when I told him I had not had the battery checked in three years. He said he would make a complaint, but I said not to bother as I had written a letter of complaint about it every week for two years. No wonder so many people die while in custody. A screw drove me to the hospital and back, which was a strange experience; he spent the whole time trying to get security information off me about what was happening on camp. He even offered me McDonald's if I talked. I told him to do one, in a jovial way, but he went to McDonald's anyway and bought himself a Big Mac.

The MOJ were still asking a lot of questions about the running of the prison. They asked the CRC department for some data. The ladies were worried; they had a look at their Key Performance Indicators and whether they were meeting them. They were miles off. I was asked to review all cases since the CRC had taken over and report it to one of the Governors. I said they would not be kind reading and I would not be involved in them cooking the stats, like they did with the ROTL stats. I spent a whole week reviewing 162 files. I made a spreadsheet and inputted all the data from every case. There was a lot of what the services would call 'soft outcomes'—this is just signposting to other services in the community. But there was not one hard outcome. Not one person was supported to obtain accommodation, employment or education directly in the nine months CRC had been in post. The manager of the CRC asked if she could sit down with me to review my report before it was sent to the Governor. I knew what this was. Damage limitation. She spent two hours doctoring my document with no input from me at all. The whole time I was sat there thinking, 'Yeah, I am the criminal'. They were defrauding public money.

The ladies in the CRC were still a liability, bless them. I moaned about the UTI long life milk I had to drink with my coffee. I knew what I was doing. They brought me a four-pint carton of milk from Waitrose every week. I wasn't predating on them or anything; they were just nice people trying to be nice. They told me they were attending an all-staff meeting. They were worried about the contract, due to the poor outcomes. I wasn't; I knew they had cooked, and would cook, the stats. After the meeting they gave me the minutes to read. They didn't have much sense when it came to security. In the minutes, they noted there had been 200 reports of absconding recently; I thought that was a low estimate. The prison decided to put a wildlife camera, with infrared and motion detectors, in the woods. It wouldn't make much of a difference, as they had no staff to go out and catch them, and even when they did go out, the screws were too scared to challenge anyone. I was sat on the phone at the end of the Greens one night. Two lads walked past me with balaclavas on and two holdalls full of stuff.

My application for weekend home leave had been submitted and would be presented to the board the following week. The Activities Hut also said they had identified a placement for me and would be doing a service visit the following week. I felt I was starting to get somewhere.

Meanwhile I was still working in the CRC office. I was doing a resettlement plan with a guy who just landed. I did this with every new arrival now. Previously CRC would only see people who requested to see them.

I asked him what his profession was prior to his conviction.

"I was a fireman."

'Good profession, do you want to return to that work post-release?'

"Probably not, I am in for Arson."

I didn't know what to say, so I asked if that made him 'Self-employed'. Thankfully, he laughed.

My application for home leave was approved! I would leave the prison on the Friday morning and return on the Sunday afternoon. I could not wait! My mate said he would pick me up and drive me back to London. He insisted. I had been talking to Kelly a lot; she wanted to come over from Ireland to spend the weekend with me. I really wanted her to be with me that weekend, too, because she had been there for me throughout, as were many others. I wasn't sure what our relationship was, at that point. I liked her a lot. She was coming over from Ireland to see me, so I guess she really liked me too. It was hard not to think about a bunk up: I had been celibate for twenty-seven months! I was a bit worried about how, if I got lucky, I would perform. I am sure most people getting out who had been in a while worried about the same.

I didn't want to go nuts on my first home leave. I wanted good food. I told everyone I was, "Going home to put on a stone." I had steak and chips for breakfast on the Friday. I also wanted to spend time with my family and Kelly. You are not allowed to drink on home leave. But fuck that, no way was I not. Just a few. It was the perfect weekend. I didn't get to see everyone I wanted to as I had so little time, but I would have more home leaves to catch up with everyone. I promised my mates the next one would be with them.

On the Monday, after I had returned, the Activities Hub told me they had found me the perfect placement. At a homeless centre in Oxford called Stepping Stones. It really was perfect. They said they would give me more details when they had them. I would be starting work within two weeks. The relief was huge. Employment, home leave, and I got my willy wet. This was what I had worked towards for over two years.

Chapter 15

Work

"What we think, we become." Buddha

I was looking forward to more home leaves and getting off the camp during the week to work. I was asked to come to the Activities Hub to discuss my placement and to complete the paperwork for ROTL to go out on weekdays to work. What they had not told me was the placement was as a volunteer. I really wanted to work, get off camp and get back into something I was so passionate about, but the fact I would not get paid was not what I needed. I told them I would dig holes, I didn't care, I just needed some money when I was released, or what chance would I have? They told me there were no paid positions currently. They said, maybe, if the centre liked me, they would offer me a paid position. I decided to take the volunteer placement, work hard and try to use my experience to support their clients. However, I told them and the OMU I still needed paid employment ASAP.

The following week my work placement was approved. The prison bus would drive a group of us into Oxford and drop us all off at our placements; everyone else's was in charity shops. I had my prison mobile on me, which could be used to track my movements. I was dropped off and told the centre was "just around the corner." It wasn't. The mobile phone provided to me had no Internet, so I just had to ask people where the centre was. I eventually found it after walking around for half an hour. But I was an hour early. It was raining, and I had no money. I had to sit on the wall outside the centre in the rain waiting for it to open. Passers-by kept telling me it was not open for another hour, and asking if I was homeless.

Eventually two people who worked at the centre turned up and gave me a coffee to warm me up. They did not know I was coming. The prison hadn't told them. The lady who ran the centre was not expecting me. She called the prison to confirm I was who I said I was. She said she used to get a lot of volunteers from the prison a year ago, but it suddenly stopped, and they were not told why. They did contact her about me but did not tell them when I was coming. Her name was Sue. She was so lovely. She did so much for the clients. Every day she would also cook for thirty to forty people. She really was a legend. She was the kind of person, if I was a secret millionaire, I would pay for a holiday for her and give her a big pay rise. I told her I used to work in the sector and would be happy to help in any way I could. It turns out, that was washing up. A lot of washing up! I wanted to get my foot in the door before telling them they were not using me to my potential. I asked if they had an advice worker. She said they had had someone from St Mungo's, but the funding ended. My first day, I was so busy. The time passed quickly. It was great to be in an environment that was not a prison, talking to people about normal things. I was exhausted when I got back to the prison. I wasn't used to any kind of labour.

At the prison the security was still a joke. A local homeless man was coming IN to the prison and sleeping on the stairwell of the Greens. He would even go to breakfast in the morning. I didn't believe my mate until he pointed him out. I spoke to the guy when I was queuing up one morning. He said the food was shit. He said he had been in Spring Hill before as a prisoner and knew how to get in to sleep on the Greens. The lads started giving him bedding and food. Not only did the screws not know who was going out the prison, they didn't know who was coming in. Shit was so bad, one of the Governors was placed on gardening leave.

The next few weeks passed quickly. In the mornings at the homeless centre, vans would turn up with loads of donated food from large stores. I would carry as much produce as I could into the centre. I had to know what the centre had lots of, so as not to take more. I had an inventory in my head. Sue would then look at what we had and make a menu. It was like a large-scale Ready Steady Cook. Between nine and noon I would help Sue with the cooking. At midday I would set up the hot plate, and then serve lunch at twelve thirty. I liked doing that bit, but then from one to three I would be washing up. Two hours every day. I have never seen so many pots, pans, plates and cutlery. Man, it was hard work.

I started to write to my probation officer in the community. I was worried. I had six months left to serve and I had no employment. Little prospect of employment on release, no accommodation and no savings at all. I continued to ask the OMU for paid work. I was told it was taking three months for work placements to be approved. It was clear I was pretty fucked, then.

I had a couple more home leaves over the next couple of months. Kelly came over again. I wanted a relationship with her when I was released, but what did I have to offer? I was feeling down. I was stressed. I wanted to pay her back for her support and love, but I had nothing to offer her. I felt I had done everything I could to not be released homeless with no prospects. My depression and anxiety attacks came back with a vengeance. One thing I had learned is, if you need help, ask for it. There is no shame in asking for help sometimes. Everyone needs help at some point in their life. I was referred to the prison counsellor, who I saw once a week. I also started to go to the RAPt groups at Spring Hill after work. Being down is my biggest trigger. I could feel the frustration building in me. Pressing the 'fuck it button' was coming.

I was getting frustrated at Stepping Stones. People would come into the centre, have food and a shower, leave, and just come back again the next day. Personally, I did not feel we were helping their situation. I requested some more meaningful work than just washing up. I asked to be allowed to try to support the clients with accommodation or access to other services, but Sue said I was needed too much in the kitchen. I asked that they ask the prison for someone else to help with the kitchen, but they just wanted me to do what I was asked to do. With no prospect of employment or anything more meaningful than washing up, my motivation disappeared. I was struggling in general. I stopped running. I was just too tired after work. I started going to acupuncture through RAPt, as they said it helped with stress. A woman in baggy trousers would put pins in my ears, and then I would lie down on big pillows and listen to whales for an hour. Every time I just got really horny, so I stopped going.

I had another home leave, which was at a bad time. Kelly was not over. I was frustrated with my situation. Not a good mix. I had a mad weekend on the piss with my mates. I drank all weekend. I didn't take cocaine, but I was tempted. The weekend was a blur. I got off the bus down the road from the prison, half drunk, half hung-over. I walked into reception and this screw who was a right jobsworth was on duty. The screws did not usually search anyone when they came back into the prison. I had never been searched once. What is the point, everyone brings stuff in over the field? This screw went through my bag with a fine tooth-comb. He found my USB stick. I would take it home with me, put films and box sets on it to watch. No big deal. I thought I would get a slap on the wrist for it. Then he started going through the pockets of my clothes in the bag. He found two pills. Two blue pills. He asked me what they were; I said I had no idea. I was genuinely confused. Then I remembered. My mate was winding me up saying I wouldn't be able to get it up after spending so long inside, so he gave me a present: two Viagra pills. I laughed it off and put them in my back pocket. I completely forgot they were there. He gave me a nicking, the prick. I think most other screws would have laughed it off. I would need to go in front of a Governor and explain why I had a USB stick and Viagra pills. I wasn't worried. I thought they would give me a loss of earnings or something.

The next morning, I went to go to work, but reception told me I had been stood down. I was not allowed to leave. The one thing I was worried about was that anyone who got a nicking, who lived on the Greens, went back to the huts. I could not deal with that now. I spoke to my counsellor, who advocated for me, but they were having none of it. I was told to move to R-hut. I hoped I could smooth it over with whoever I would see for my nicking. I was wrong. I was stood in front of a senior officer. I pleaded guilty but explained why I had the pills; I had no intention of bringing them back with me, I mean why would I? This guy goes into one, saying I had put the security of the prison at risk and brought in drugs, he even had a go because porn was on the USB stick. I mean, come on! He went to town on me, adding on charges. I was to be stood down for two months, loss of earnings for a month. That means no more work and no more home leaves. I knew the two months stood down would, in reality, be three or four months as it takes so long to get your applications to the board. I might have one more home leave before being released. I was suspicious of the search and sentence. Did I create too much fuss about getting out for paid work? Did my criticism of CRC make me a target? I didn't know, and I suppose it didn't matter.

I don't know if I was targeted. But if I was, and if their plan was to keep me quiet, it did not work. I now had nothing to do or lose. I appealed the decision. I was told I was lucky not to be put back into closed conditions, and it was dismissed. I didn't see the difference now. I knew of people who were caught with mobile phones who were still getting ROTLs. I was told I could have my old job back at the CRC. They seemed to be surprised when I told them to shove it. For over two years I had behaved, bit my tongue, and got on with it. Not any longer. I decided I would spend the last part of my sentence being a pain in the arse. I refused to work. I decided I would be a man of leisure. You are not allowed to sleep or lay on your bed during the day. Good luck trying to stop me. If a screw did come onto the huts and challenge me I just told them to fuck off. This is what happens when you have absolutely nothing to lose. I was sharing a room with an old Muslim guy. He was sound. He taught me about stocks and the stock market; he was minted—his confiscation order was forty-seven million pounds. He was arrested for insider trading. He said I read a lot, but I read the wrong things, I should read things that would make me money. He gave me a book about the stock market to read, which I did. He did subject me to hours of Arabic box sets though. They were like Arabic Game of Thrones. He loved them.

I fucked everything off for a few weeks. The business course, RAPt, counselling. I was told I was sabotaging everything. They were having a laugh. They knew and I knew I had been let down. Yes, I got a nicking, but it did not change anything really. They knew and I knew I would be leaving with absolutely nothing.

All my mates had now either been released or were out volunteering during the day. I spent my days reading, running and sunbathing. The screws hated me now. I just did not give a fuck. I would sunbathe all afternoon. That wasn't allowed either. It was at this point I met Tony. He had come over from HMP Grendon, which was next door. He and his firm did a big robbery in Kings Cross dressed as police officers, robbing them of computer chips. They even had a police van and Alsatian dogs. They turned up at the warehouse with blue lights flashing, told security that there was someone on the roof and they needed access to the CCTV. They then tie them up and rob the place. He had so many stories. I would go to his room every day and have a cuppa with him just to hear them. I had found an ally. Tony was angry at the system. He had been through it many times before and said it was worse than ever and Spring Hill was the worst he had experienced in terms of resettlement. He had been in and out of prison his whole adult life, but he wanted to make system changes. He took my old job at CRC. If they thought I was a pain, Tony was like a dog with a bone when he saw what was going on. He did not give a shit. He started writing letters to anyone he could think of. Our biggest issue was the number of people being released homeless from the prison. The funding and resources were in place. There was no need for it. It was a lack of knowledge and will to change it. Tony was brought in front of the Governor to be read the riot act. Tony had none of it. The mad fucker wrote a complaint against the Governor, saying the Governor had made threats against him, and he had bad breath.

I did enjoy getting funny stories from the lads when they came back at night to the camp. Bear had been working in a local gym. At the end of the first week, they rang the prison to say they couldn't have him back as he was "Too aggressive to work with the public, he is scaring them."

Spring Hill was on BBC news that week. A lad who was a Muslim convert had absconded. He was getting a bit radical. Saying stupid shit on camp, although no one really took him seriously as he was a melt, but he was talking about going to Syria when released. But one day he fucked off.

They had a picture of him on the national news. They were obviously worried he could be involved in a terror attack or get to Syria while on the run.

I was quite enjoying doing fuck all. My worker at RAPt who I agreed to work with again told me I was having a 'Dry relapse', the mad fucker. I was stupidly honest with her, telling her my motivation was low and it was exhausting being positive all the time. She spoke to my counsellor and upped my appointments with him. At least she did her job, to be fair to her, something I had seen little of at Spring Hill.

There were a lot of steroids on camp at that time. Everyone was roided up; the aggression was high, lots of fights, which were not common. My RAPt worker asked me if I was doing them as my demeanour had changed, and I was training again too, but doing weights. I hadn't been taking anything. Fuck that stuff. There was a football match every Sunday morning on the field. That week, the game was suspended after twenty minutes, as so many bad tackles and fights were breaking out, proper roid-rage. Some of the lads were taking Crystal Meth too, which really did not help things. The camp was a melting pot waiting to explode.

A couple of days later, a couple of black lads robbed a Muslim lad's room. All hell broke loose. About fifty Muslim lads went to the black lads' hut and smashed them all up. Two got stabbed. Big race war. The prison was on lockdown for the next twenty-four hours. This happened all the time in Wanno, but never here. The following day healthcare was open for a 'Knife-wound amnesty' so people could get treatment for stab wounds without the screws knowing about it.

I started writing to the Inside Times again about what was happening with people being released from Spring Hill with little chance of not being recalled. How can you not when you are released homeless, with no job or savings? I started to tell mates the letters were from me. They dubbed me the 'Zodiac'. There was a guy on camp who everyone hated. He was a plastic screw, so I started signing the letters in his name.

Tony had been going to church a lot and he was to be baptised at the prison. Tony and his mate were trying to get me to go to church with them, but I was having none of that nonsense. But I said I would go to his baptism. What a freak show that was. I met the pastor, who was American. He said he would pray for my salvation, the lunatic. They put up a big inflatable pool in the games room and filled it with water; it took them hours. Tony had his family there, it was nice hearing him talking about his love for his daughters, and I am glad finding God helped him. Then Tony and the pastor got in the inflatable bath and the pastor dunked him under the water. I found it all a bit mental. Up next was Tony's mate. I didn't know him very well. But he was stood in the inflatable bath telling everyone he has changed and found God. As he is about to get dunked into the water, the guy next to me chuckles to himself and says, "Do you know what he is in for?" I say I don't. He says, "For drowning his mother in the bath." We both laughed out loud and got an angry stare from the pastor.

Chapter 16

Release

"At the end of every hard-earned day-people find some reason to believe." Bruce Springsteen

During my incarceration the world was changing. There was to be a referendum on whether the UK should leave the European Union. I was very much a Remainer. I felt there was no chance the British public would vote to leave. Spring Hill was to hold a Newsnight-style event, inviting academic speakers and the local community. It would be recorded and televised. I found it all rather ironic, as we were asked to provide questions and attend the event even though none of us could vote in the election. I was well-read on the subject as I had read all the newspapers I could get my hands on every day for the past two years. I submitted a question about how Article 50 would be invoked. On the night of the event there were a lot of people from the community in the dining room on camp. The TV cameras had been set up. Us cons took our seats. The panel introduced themselves and the questions began. It was clear they had no idea how the referendum would play out and how the result, whatever it was, would affect the UK. My name was read out and I asked my question about invoking Article 50. The panel looked shocked that I had any idea what Article 50 was. All the press reports were about the referendum and not so much about how any vote to leave could be achieved if this is what the public voted for. One of the panel said I had asked a question even academics had no answers for, as Article 50 had never been used before. I followed that up with a question on the Irish backstop and how a leave deal could be achieved in the two-year notice period. After the debate a lovely young lady who was studying criminology and politics at Cambridge approached me. She asked me where I was from and my background. I chatted to her for about an hour as the TV crew packed up. She asked for my number, and we laughed about that. I gave her my e-mail address, which would probably be the only thing that worked of mine when I was released. It was clear she was after a bit of rough. It was good to know I still had it and could nick a bird.

It was around this time I joined a band. Spring Hill had a music studio; however, it was impossible to get in there unless you were a rapper, from what I could tell. I met a guy called Wayne who I saw playing the guitar one day. We had a chat about bands we liked. He had written an amazing song about prison and his relationship with his girlfriend, my favourite line being, "She told me she had a designer vagina, when I lifted up her clit, it said, 'Made in China." He invited me to come into the studio with him. I would just sit there and listen to him record. But there was a group of lads who were in a rock band. Their singer had been released, so they just jammed. I was messing about one day and I started singing lyrics to a Joy Division song and they joined in. It wasn't half bad, and I started dreaming of international stardom. What is more rock'n'roll than to have a band formed in prison? I loved it, but the lead guitarist, probably the only one of us with any actual talent, got a job in a charity shop and I started an advanced Excel IT course. Not the rock'n'roll ending I was hoping for.

I was randomly called to see the Governor. I had no idea why. I went up to the top floor of the big house and he was sat in his little office in the corner. He didn't let me sit down. He said he'd had reports from officers about my behaviour. I had submitted a weekend home leave request four weeks prior to my release date. He started laying in to me a bit; it felt like he wanted a reaction from me. I was calm, but I explained the reason for the change in my behaviour and why I felt the way I did. I explained I was frustrated at the system. I said I was worried I would be walking out of Spring Hill in two months with absolutely nothing. He said this did not happen; I laughed. We both knew this happened every day. He said he would not sign off my application for home leave unless my behaviour changed. I reminded him I had two months left to serve and this was no longer a carrot he could dangle in front of me. He threatened to send me back to enclosed conditions. I asked if this was due to my behaviour, which was mild, or for his stats? This seemed to infuriate him, and his fat little face went bright red. He shouted at me and told me to get out of his office. I left not knowing if I would be ghosted out back to enclosed conditions. I didn't care.

I continued to write to my probation officer in the community about my resettlement needs, with no response at all. As I was relatively close to release, the CRC now allowed me to use the phone to call the probation office. My worker was always off. She had more time off than Santa Claus. I was told she had been off sick for six months. I asked if they had checked she hadn't died.

Despite the ROTL situation improving, there was still a lot of absconding. There were three in one night. I knew two lads who went out every night. They would go to local pubs and restaurants. But one night they set off a sensor in the woods, so the screws did a random check on all prisoners. It was late, so a lot of people were asleep in bed. The next day only one of the lads got a nicking. The other had made a manikin and put it in his bed, Alcatraz style. Absolute Genius.

As Bear was back on camp and no longer working in the gym he started training other cons, charging a pound for a session with him. Other people paid, but he came up to me and said, "You have done really well to train yourself, you are fit, but you now need someone to push you to help you tone up." I said I didn't want pushing. His reply was "Fuck off, you fat cunt." He would come to my room and wake me up at six thirty to do circuits. Bear wasn't the kind of guy you said no to. I hoped he did not use his unique motivational skills on the lads who were paying him though.

The application for my last weekend home leave before release was, to my absolute amazement, approved. I only arranged to see my sons. I would spend the rest of my time looking for job opportunities and accommodation. My sister was due to have a baby; there was just no room for me at my parents' house, where she lived too. I wanted to see Kelly, but I needed to sort my life out. I had no chance of doing it while in Spring Hill. I couldn't even get on the Internet. How can you apply for anything at all without Internet access? Post a written job application? I was sent on a course pre-release about how to get jobs again. It was the same woman I'd clashed with when I first arrived. I attended, but I said I would not be changing my mind on applying for jobs in the homeless sector. She had a list of jobs for people to apply for in the local community. Not one person on the course was from the local community.

My weekend home leave was great, but it made me realise the huge battle I had in front of me. Up to now I'd been worried about how I would get through my sentence; now I was worried how I would get through being released. While home, I had applied for housing with my local authority. They informed me I was not priority need and they had no duty to house me. I expected this. But I asked for a deposit loan so I could rent privately. They said they had no such scheme. I approached my previous housing provider; they did not give me the time of day. Again I expected this. I returned to Spring Hill with no housing options at all. I was due for release in four weeks. What I did return with was a job advert, for a position at a homeless hostel in Westminster. It was an entry-level position, but I had a lot to prove, and trust to rebuild. I went to the OMU office and showed them the advert. I requested day release so I could go to an Internet café and apply for the job. If the approval of the home leave was a surprise, their response to this application was too. It was declined. I just could not get the rationale behind the decision. I spoke to my OMU officer; he said I was wasting my time applying for that particular position, as the position came with a DBS check. I reminded him I had to disclose my conviction anyway. I appealed the decision, but it was refused again. I had to come up with a plan again to get around the sheer ridiculousness of 'Resettlement' at Spring Hill. I wrote a handwritten application. Applications in the homeless sector are long. It's not just sending in a CV. I posted it to a mate, and he kindly applied for the position for me online. My conviction and current abode were disclosed. Two weeks later, I received a letter inviting me for an interview. I flew up to the OMU with the letter confirming the interview in hand. I felt I had proved something to them. Afterwards, I found the lady doing the employment course and showed her the letter. I wanted to show her she was wrong too. She said, "They won't give you the job, it just looks good for them letting you apply for it."

I submitted the paperwork for day release to attend the interview. Surely, they could not refuse this one.

In the meantime, I was still attending my advanced Excel course. It was like learning a new language. One of the lads on the course was late as he had a healthcare appointment. He walks in and shouts, "I don't have HIV, I just have chlamydia!" while high-fiving everyone. He sits next to me and says, "Don't worry, nobody minds the invisible man at a dinner party." I spent the next ten minutes trying to work out what the fuck it meant. During the break he came to talk to me again, clearly not finished telling me about his STI. "I know the slag I got it from, I fucked her like four years ago, but she has had four kids since then." I can see the cogs turning in his head. "They told me to contact everyone I had sex with, but what about the kids?" I asked what he meant. "Will the kids have chlamydia?" he asked. I said to him. "Whatever the fuck you do, do not call her and say you have chlamydia and she should get her kids tested too!" I see him later that night with loads of OL (outgoing letter) free postage envelopes in his hand. He tells me they are to write to all the women in Luton he had fucked.

My application for ROTL to attend my job interview was approved. The prison bus was to take me to Oxford station, where I would catch a train to Marylebone in London, then jump on the tube from there to Victoria. I applied for a travel warrant, which was also arranged, as I had no money. I had brought shirt and trousers back with me from my home leave, just in case I needed them for such an occasion. I didn't bother doing the usual paperwork for it to be added to my property list, as I would get it in time for my funeral if I was lucky.

On the morning of my interview I presented at reception to be told the prison bus had left without me. I was clearly pissed off; so one of the better screws said he would drive me to the station. I signed my ROTL licence, a piece of paper with a little photo of me on it and the reason I was allowed to leave prison for the day. We arrived at the station; the screw waved me off and wished me good luck. I went to the ticket window and showed them the travel warrant from the prison, which would be exchanged for return train tickets. The attendant said he could not give me the tickets, as the date was wrong on the form. He was right, the date was wrong. He said he couldn't edit it, and apologised. I stood outside the station having no idea what to do. The prison was not due to collect me for five hours. I had my prison phone, but I had no credit. Now I really was pissed off. I had managed to get an interview for a job despite getting no help from the prison, and now they couldn't even complete the paperwork to get me there. As I was standing in the rain cursing the prison, a coach pulled up full of some Asian tourists who had been to

Bicester Village shopping. As there were so many of them the station assistant opened a little gate to the platform for them. I saw it as a sign. Fuck it. I decided to try to get to the interview by bunking there and back. If I got caught, I would just blame the prison. I got on the train to Marylebone and hid in the toilet when I saw the ticket guy coming down the aisle. When I arrived at Marylebone, I had to get past the ticket barriers. I saw a lady with loads of bags, so I offered to help her. Again, they opened a little gate and I just walked through with her. I helped her to a taxi, and she thanked me and said I was a "Good man." If only she knew.

I now needed to get on the tube; I didn't have the time to get a bus. I got caught trying to get through a gate this time. I told the ticket guy I had just been released from prison and I needed to get to my probation appointment, or they would recall me, and I had no money to buy a ticket. I pulled the ROTL paper out of my pocket and showed him the top of it with my photo and HMP Spring Hill on the top. He looked scared; he just opened the gate for me. At Victoria I did the same and it worked. I had managed to get to my interview despite all the barriers put in front of me. I was quite proud of myself.

As I sat in reception at the hostel waiting to be called for my interview, I met some of the residents and got chatting to them. I wanted to return to this kind of job, as I loved supporting others. It was my vocation. I was called down to the offices to be interviewed by two ladies, who were nice. I spoke about my experience in the homeless sector prior to my arrest and what I had done while in prison to support others. I felt the interview was going well, I seemed to have a good rapport with the two ladies. But then I was asked, "What do you think about PIE?" This stumped me, and I had to admit I had no idea what PIE was. When they told me it meant Psychologically Informed Environments and explained the term, I spoke about the work we did at a specialist hostel in Hammersmith which I felt was PIE before it was coined PIE. At this point, one of the ladies said, "Did you used to work at Market Lane hostel?" Shit! My biggest worry was, even with my disclosure, that the reputation I knew I had in the sector as the manager jailed for drug charges would haunt me. I couldn't lie; Market Lane was on my CV. So, I said 'Yes I did'. I felt my heart sink. The lady said, "I remember you, you spoke at a health meeting so passionately about health in homelessness. You inspired me to bring some of your ideas back to another project I was working in." I thanked her and said I would show this same passion if I was given the opportunity to work with them. They said they would be in touch. I wanted to say that would be difficult for them, but it didn't seem the right thing to say. I spent some more time at reception saying goodbye to the residents, and said I hoped to see them again soon.

My journey back was much the same as the way to London. I just flashed my prison paperwork at gates and barriers were opened. I didn't even hide in the toilet when the ticket attendant came. I explained what had happened. I provided the prison contact info and told him to contact them. I didn't tell the prison about their fuck-up and my adventures. They would probably add fare evasion charges to my sentence.

Four days later, I had not heard anything. I called home and my sister, who was checking my e-mails for me, said I had one from one of the ladies who interviewed me asking me to call her. I went straight to the Activities Hub to call her. I was nervous. The outcome was important for my future. I suddenly felt a bit silly applying for it. I could hear the employment lady in my head. "They only interviewed you so it looks good for them. You won't get the job." I reached Natalie, the manager of the hostel, who had interviewed me. I apologised for any delay calling her back. She apologised for the wait too. They had said they would let me know their decision the next day. The fact I had not heard anything till now did not bode well, I felt. Natalie said, "You came across confident and happy." I wasn't sure either was true, but good start. She said my interview was "very accomplished, and your experience was evident." I was waiting for the "Thank you for applying but…" Instead she said, "I really wanted to take you on," I interjected and said I understood it was not a conventional application and thanked her for considering me. She then said, "The reason for the delay was, I have been trying to sell you to our HR department. You can imagine this is not an easy sell." I felt that was it, I was again waiting for something like, "We would like you to apply in the future when you are more settled." In my mind, that was it, she was being polite and letting me down easy. But she said, "When can you start?!"

I was completely taken aback. You know when someone says, "It felt like a ton of bricks was taken off my back"? That was exactly how it felt. I became a bumbling idiot thanking Natalie. I said she would not regret it and I would repay her faith in me. I thanked her for fighting my corner. Not even my brief did that. I said I was due to be released on the 2nd of September. A Friday. I said I could start on the Monday. She laughed and asked if I didn't need a period to adjust. I said I didn't, that I was keen to get on with my life. We agreed to discuss a start date at another time. She said I would need to provide documents for a DBS check before I could start. I said I would be in with them ASAP. I thanked her another ten times and I said I would see her soon.

I was ecstatic. I didn't know who to call first. I must have used twenty pounds phone credit calling everyone to tell them my good news. It was the start of me repaying everyone for their support. All I could do to repay them was to learn from my mistakes, not make them again, and get myself back on my feet.

I saw the employment lady a few days later. I couldn't help but gloat. I had proved her wrong. I said I hoped she had learned something and would stop telling people they could not do something. She just sniggered at me. I didn't care, fuck her.

I had seventeen days left to serve. I now had a job. But I didn't have anywhere to live.

The next day I was asked via the tannoy system to go to the prison officers' office. I had never heard my name on the tannoy before, it was quite disconcerting. I couldn't work out why they wanted to see me. I went to the office in the centre of the prison where you collect post. I was greeted by a senior officer I had never talked to before. We went to his office and he told me to sit down. He said, "Don't worry, you are not in trouble; we review everyone who is due for release. I read your NOMIS and I wanted to meet you." OK, I thought, random... He said, "Your NOMIS is quite unique. You have a lot of positive entries over the past few years. More than most would. But you also have a lot of negative entries. This does not normally happen. It is usually one or the other." I was smiling. I was pretty fucking proud to be honest. He started reading some of the entries to himself; he was laughing. He said "You are quick and witty; I will give you that." Big smile on my face. He said it was clear I was a good guy, but it was also clear I was angry. He said if I carried this with me, it would only affect me in the future. He said I could not go through life with that attitude. I said I was not angry before coming to prison. He asked me to explain why I was angry. I went into a long rant about the police, the court system, the prison system, the lack of resettlement. I said I felt I had done everything that was asked of me for nearly three years. I behaved myself. I did not get involved in anything. I did courses, I fully engaged with any support on offer. And here I was days from release with no resettlement at all. I told him about getting a job but explained the barriers I faced getting that job. He listened. He actually apologised. I felt like this was the only conversation of any real substance I had with a professional in three years. I thanked him for giving me the opportunity to tell my story and frustrations and for listening. He walked around his desk, looked me in the eye and said, "Don't come back, leave that anger at the gate. I wish you the best of luck" and shook my hand. As I left the office, I went for a walk around the field. There and then I decided he was right, and I had to let it go. All of it. Even the blame I placed on myself. I could not let it affect my future. Once I walked out the gate, I had to leave the whole experience in the past and not dwell on it. Again, it felt like another ton of bricks was taken off my back.

The following day, I was called on the tannoy again to go to the big house, to see the Governor this time. Suddenly everyone wanted to speak to me. I was ready for an argument. I had submitted a complaint about my lack of resettlement as a last "fuck you". This time the Governor asked me to sit down. He said, "Are you going to do anything stupid?" I said he needed to be more specific. He said it was clear I was frustrated, and he was concerned I would act on this. He then said, "You have a lot of influence on camp, (I didn't) are you going to use that to be disruptive? To be honest I can't afford the bus to send you back to an enclosed prison for the last few days of your sentence." I asked if he had responded to my complaint. He said this was the response. I had said to myself I had to let it all go after the chat with the screw. So, I said I was angry, but I had no intention of being disruptive. He thanked me and said, "Can I ask a favour?" I laughed and said he was pushing it. He said, "Can you talk to Tony and ask him to end his campaign against the prison. You can be reasonable; he is making life very difficult for us." I was proud of Tony. I said I would speak to him if he approved a ROTL for me to drop some documents in to my new employer in London and he agreed. And true to his word, it was approved the next day. I went to see Tony and said, "Keep up the good work mate, you are getting somewhere, the Gov ask me to speak to you, to ask you to cool it down. Fuck that cunt, fancy writing a letter to the housing minister? I have an address we can send it to." Tony was bouncing off the walls, more motivated than ever to carry on his campaign.

Time started to drag like a snake's cock. I just wanted out. I was bouncing around camp though, knowing my time was coming to an end. I had another new cellmate. I think by this point I had had more cellmates than Nelson Mandela. Andy was a sixty-two-year-old guy who looked forty. A life of crime may not pay but it does wonders for ageing. Andy told me he was in for GBH. How many sixty-two-year-olds get done for GBH? Andy was hard as it comes though, ex-military. Old-school Scottish guy. He was fit as fuck but was only five foot five. He told me his ex-partner sent three blokes round to his house to weigh him in after a falling out. Two of the guys had knives and one had a bat. Andy fought them, the mad fucker, disarmed them and smashed fuck out of them. He was arrested and sentenced to twelve years! Now I am no legal adviser, but how the fuck can someone be found guilty if three guys have come at him with weapons? Even my brief would get him off. But he was told he did not react with reasonable force and that his military background made him a weapon. I didn't want to question Andy too much as I just could not believe this was true. He must have seen in my face I didn't believe him, so he showed me his court papers. I didn't read them all, but he was true to his word. He did also bite a copper's ear off, though, which he had failed to mention. I said it was like the script to Con Air.

I was planning what I was going to do the day and weekend I was released. You daydream about that day you are released all through your sentence. It was my son's 16th birthday on the day of my release. I was expected to present at probation, which for me was in Hounslow where my old flat was. I requested a move to Askew Road probation in Shepherd's Bush, but it was refused. I also requested I present on the Monday so I could see my son in Hemel Hempstead on his birthday. This was also refused. Good start to my journey with probation for the next three years. I had arranged drinks with friends on the Saturday, to thank everyone for their support. I couldn't buy a round, but hey. I sent invites out via letter, like it was from the royals. I was careful to call it a 'Getting out party' and not a 'Coming out party'.

I spent my last few days with people I now called friends. Promising we would all stay in touch when they were released. We all had something in common, a life experience many don't share. Oscar and I made grand plans to tear up the King's Road. He had another six months to serve, but I knew we would remain friends.

Tony made me promise I would carry on the campaign for prison reform in the community. He had his own grand plans. It was clear this was only the start of his campaign.

Bear told me I was an annoying Gooner cunt and he never wanted to see me again.

The day before my release I gave away all my possessions. It is amazing how much stuff you can collect in prison. All I wanted to keep were letters sent to me. I gave all my stuff to lifers or lads with IPP (Imprisonment for Public Protection) sentences. They needed it more. I could have sold my PlayStation, stereo, and a new USB stick for quite a few quid, but I wouldn't need burn and tuna when I got home.

I was told to report to the OMU to complete my release paperwork. I was asked for a release address. I reminded them they had failed to source accommodation for me. My OMU worker said, "We have to have an address for the system,"' and I said they should have thought about that when I said I would be leaving homeless. He said, "We can take any address – parents, friends, family – we need to have one for the system." It was then I realised how the stats were cooked for the numbers released homeless: people gave any address, so then the system did not identify as them as being released homeless. I dug my heels in and said no. I insisted they record: No fixed abode. I was told this would likely delay my release the following day as I could be waiting hours at reception for my paperwork to be signed off. I might miss my son's birthday party if this was true. But I had to do what I felt was right. I said I would happily wait.

I never slept a wink that night. I was excited, anxious, worried, and horny.

I had a few kind offers to pick me up on the day of my release, but I refused them: I wanted to walk down that hill and make my way back to London by myself as a free man. I went to reception at 9am. A group of mates were there waiting for me to wave me off. Bear was there, said he wanted to make sure I was leaving. I would miss the lads. I said my goodbyes and went into reception anticipating they would make it difficult for me. They couldn't give a fuck; they had my licence ready to sign. They gave me forty-seven pounds and that was it. I was free.

I swung my prison holdall over my shoulder and I slowly walked down the hill, surrounded by the Buckinghamshire countryside. I let out a big sigh, thinking about my arrest, conviction and a thirty-three-month prison stay, and I thought, 'What good do you think you do?'

Epilogue

I think it is relevant to ask why I wrote this book. I think if you told people who know me that I had written a book, they would probably laugh at you. At first, writing the book was for me, to finalise a difficult period in my life and to try to make sense of it all. It was the hardest time of my life, which I would not have got through without the unconditional support of my amazing family and friends. I felt it would be therapeutic to write it down, to share my experience. I also wanted my sons to read it. Maybe it is a way to ask for their forgiveness and understanding. I hope they also learn from it and don't make the mistakes that I did. It was more difficult to write, in an emotional sense, than I expected. It has brought back a lot of feelings, both good and bad.

When I started the book I wanted to write about some of the funny people and stories from prison and how I used humour to get through it; you can find humour, kindness and friends in the darkest of places and situations. But there are some serious issues that I have written about. I can't write a book about prison without writing about the need for prison reform. The more I wrote, the more I realised that, although this book is not supposed to be a book about system change in the prison system, it is, in fact, about that. And if I don't try to offer my view and highlight the dire situation this country's prisoners face, I would be letting them all down. I can use this book as a platform to discuss change.

It is important to note how lucky I was. Stay with me. Many people enter the prison system with no support from friends and family. Many have addictions and mental health problems. I had these but not to the level which the vast majority of others have who go to prison. I was also lucky to have co-defendants who looked out for me. I was also lucky enough to have friends who were already in prison. I wouldn't say I was protected, but I was guided, and as a result I escaped relatively unscathed. It is difficult to quantify what effect prison had on me. I like to think I am a stronger and wiser person as a result. I am mentally stronger. I now feel I can get through anything. But, how has it affected me? I think the biggest thing is my mistrust of authority. I do not trust the police. I would not engage with the police in any circumstances now. I wrote about letting it all go. But I can't get past this mistrust. I have tried, but if anything, it has grown. My experience is that the police want convictions, not to investigate. They have a narrative they form, often based on wrong information, and run with that narrative. They don't consider alternatives. They start from the basis that someone is guilty, not innocent, and try to prove that guilt. Something I learned a few months after my conviction was that on the morning the police raided my flat, they also raided another flat that they had intelligence on, as part of the conspiracy I was involved in. (I wasn't, but anyway). During this raid they found one kilo of cocaine. The person whose flat it was, was not even arrested. This was all disclosed during another trial that took place while I was in prison. I am happy for the guy who didn't get arrested, good luck to him. But why he was not even arrested, and I was arrested and convicted, I will never know.

I will let you, reading this, decide if I should have gone to prison for what I did. I broke the law. I deserved to be punished. What I would like you to consider is, was my sentence a fitting one, and was there an alternative to sending me to prison for thirty-three months? It costs the UK taxpayer on average £33.5k a year to imprison someone. It cost the taxpayer approximately £100k to imprison me. I was not a risk to the public. My conviction was not for violence. I was working when I was arrested, providing a public service as well as paying tax. As an alternative, I could have remained in the community. Working, with an electronic tag, with a curfew, for thirty-three months. With weekly probation appointments and drug tests. I would have kept my flat and I could even have done community service on weekends. If I did not adhere to these conditions, then send me to prison. Prison should be the last option. Some may feel this a soft approach, but having no freedom in the community is not soft. I would have learned the same lessons and I would have cost the taxpayers next to nothing, and I would have been paying tax and contributing to society. Between 1993 and 2012, the prison population in England and Wales doubled to 86,000. This must be addressed. Alternative sentencing must be addressed now.

So, what has happened since I was released? I could write another book on the probation service. Jesus, if I thought dealing with screws was hard and the prison system was in crisis, fuck me, probation services are a joke. They also did everything they could to try and make my life hard. Every interaction I had with them was an absolute mind fuck. I thought once I was released it was over, ohhh no, thirty-three months of probation. I had more probation officers than I had cellmates.

I managed not to reoffend and be recalled. I threw myself into my career. I started working in the job I got while in Spring Hill, two weeks after being released. I have since progressed back into a management role, receiving two awards for my work with the homeless.

I stayed with my parents and friends for a few months, sleeping on floors and sofas until I saved enough to rent somewhere. I moved to Hemel Hempstead for a while to be closer to my sons but needed to move back after a few months to work in London.

Things never worked out with Kelly. I wish I'd tried harder to make it work.

Oscar and I remain friends and did indeed tear up the King's Road.

I don't take drugs anymore, But, I do enjoy a beer still.

I have had no further interactions with the Italian or Albanian mafia.

Acknowledgements:

I have a lot of people to thank, for both their support while I was in prison and who were part of me deciding to write a book about my experience. In no particular order.

Andy wrote to me every week without fail while I was inside. Probably over 150 letters as he sometimes wrote more than one a week. Andy kept all the letters I sent him, and gave them back to me last year. The result of doing that is this book.

Liz kindly edited the book for me pro bono. Which was no small task I can tell you. Thank you so much.

Jenny T. Without her support and character reference I may have never got back into the homeless sector. I hope I have gone some way to paying you back.

Martin was there for not only me, but my sons too. I will never forget that.

Sam. Thanks for being cool.

I have so many good friends, who stayed with me during my ordeal. Thanks so much for the postal orders and visits! I really can't thank you all enough.

Kim, Aly, Jon-jo, Tom & Jenny, Jamie, Trevor, Amanda, Rebecca, Danielle & Sam.

Thank you all.

Lastly, My amazing family. I love you all. I won't do it again, I promise!

Printed in Great Britain
by Amazon